Materials Science
FIBERS

making use of the secrets of matter

◈ *Atlantic Europe Publishing*

First published in 2003 by
Atlantic Europe Publishing Company Ltd.

Author
Brian Knapp, BSc, PhD

Art Director
Duncan McCrae, BSc

Senior Designer
Adele Humphries, BA, PGCE

Editors
Mary Sanders, BSc, and Gillian Gatehouse

Illustrations
David Woodroffe

Design and production
EARTHSCAPE EDITIONS

Scanning and retouching
Global Graphics sro, Czech Republic

Print
LEGO SpA, Italy

Materials Science – Volume 7: Fibers
A CIP record for this book is available from the British Library

ISBN 1 86214 321 8

Acknowledgments
The publishers would like to thank the following for their kind
help and advice: *Susan J. Beates*; *The Drake Well Museum,
Commonwealth of Pennsylvania Historical and Museum
Commission for the oil samples page 31*; *Christine Gater*; *David M.
Graham and Robert A. (Robin) Graham*; *Jessica, Josephine, and
Valerie Hargreaves*; *Henley Hot Air Balloons*; *Bill Knapp*; *Richard
and Emma Lundberg*; *Royal Berkshire Fire and Rescue Service*;
Pete Thompson; *Wing King Tong Co., Ltd*; *Barbara T. Zolli*.

Picture credits
All photographs are from the Earthscape Editions photolibrary
except the following: (c=center t=top b=bottom l=left r=right)

NASA 51t.

*This product is manufactured from sustainable managed forests.
For every tree cut down, at least one more is planted.*

Contents

(*Left*) Velcro® strip holding computer cables in place.

1: The nature of fibers

A FIBER is a slender THREAD or STRAND of material. It appears so fragile that you could be forgiven for thinking that it had no use at all. But a spider uses it to make a web so tough it will hold a fly, we use it to make the clothes we wear, and parachutists put their whole lives at risk and rely entirely on the special properties of fibers.

So how could such slender threads have found a place that is central to our lives? The answer lies in the fact that a fiber is much more than it appears to be.

Just as a chain appears to be no more than a thread when seen from afar, so a thread is far more complicated than it appears to be to the human eye.

The key to understanding everything about threads is to know that they are nearly all made of molecules arranged in a very special way. Fibers contain what are known as GIANT MOLECULES and are made of simple repeating patterns of ATOMS bound together in such a way as to give a fiber incredible strength, flexibility, and elasticity. We will look at how molecules are linked together on page 10.

Fibers and filaments

There are two kinds of threads or strands of material. When you talk about a fiber, you are talking about a thread that has a definite length. Cotton is a fiber formed in the cotton seed (boll). An extremely long (effectively endless) strand of material, as made by a silkworm or in a factory, is more accurately called a FILAMENT.

(*Above and right*) A spider sends out a fine, never-ending sticky thread, or filament, as it makes its web. These filaments, often referred to as "silk," are made inside the animal's body and pushed out through a tiny opening in the abdomen. This process is called extrusion, and it produces a single filament that is as long as the spider wants to make it. Filaments of this kind are made of proteins.

See **Vol. 1: Plastics** to find out more about sheets of material.

(*Below*) The world contains a bewildering variety of fibers. Some are natural, such as the spider's web opposite; others are entirely a result of human effort in a chemical factory. But nearly all of them have this in common: They are made of long chains of molecules with carbon running along their "backbones."

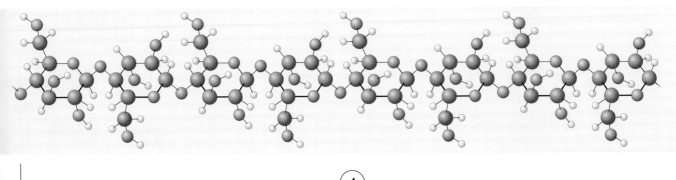

Whether they are fibers or filaments, they are very long compared with their width. This shape is what distinguishes them from a sheet of the same material.

A human hair is about 90 microns across (a micron is short for micrometer, which is a millionth of a meter). You can use this to judge the thickness of all other fibers and filaments. Silk, for example, is about 5 microns across, while a glass fiber used for sending messages may be about 10 microns across. Wool fibers are usually 16 to 40 microns. By the time fibers reach 150 microns across, they are getting less flexible and are called bristles.

(*Below*) Fiber diameters compared.

KEY

Human hair 90 microns

Fiberglass 14 microns

Typical optical fiber 10 microns

Silk 5 microns

Thinnest glass microfiber 0.1 of a micron

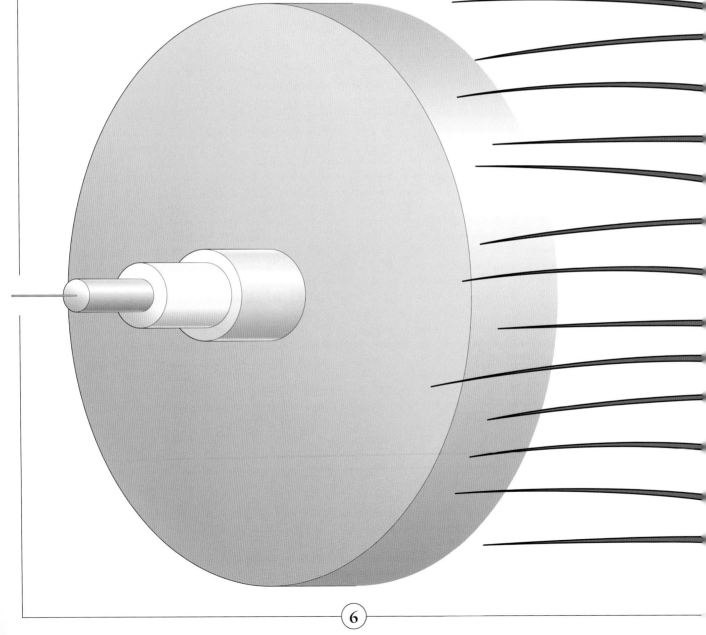

See **Vol. 5: Glass** *to find out more about glass fibers.*

See **Vol. 6: Dyes, paints, and adhesives** *for more on dyeing fibers.*

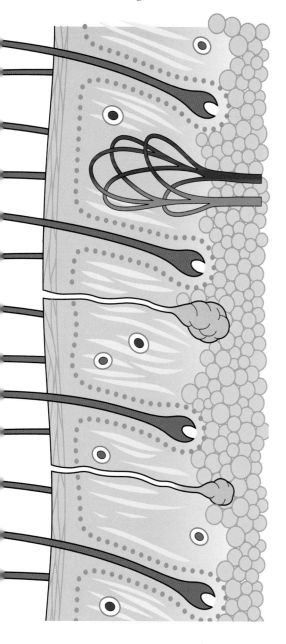

(*Below*) Hair is produced inside a special group of cells that make up the hair follicle. It pushes outward through the skin.

Fiber qualities

All fibers have qualities that make them useful. Nearly all fibers are strong when pulled. They are said to have good TENSILE (PULLING) STRENGTH. Fibers are also flexible, meaning they can be bent without breaking, and many are elastic, meaning they will stretch when pulled and then go back to their original size when released.

But many fibers also have limitations. For example, some will melt at low temperatures. Others will not melt but DECOMPOSE to black carbon, a process called CHARRING. Some fibers absorb water, swell, and get heavy when wet. They may also become weaker when wet. Others do not absorb water at all and so are difficult to DYE with the more common water-based dyes. Some natural fibers are readily attacked by bacteria, fungi, or insects. Others begin to decompose in light or heat.

This list of possible limitations should not suggest to you that fibers are really poor materials. It simply shows that you need to pick and choose the fiber you want for the purpose you have in mind. For example, cotton actually gets stronger when wet, and synthetic fibers do not suffer from attacks by fungus or insects.

Natural and artificial fibers

For thousands of years people have used NATURAL FIBERS, that is, fibers from plants and animals.

When people deal with natural fibers, they are simply making the naturally occurring fibers into new patterns by the processes of SPINNING and WEAVING. They are mechanical processes. No chemical change is involved.

The world of ARTIFICIAL FIBERS (which includes, but is not the same as, SYNTHETIC FIBERS, as you will learn below) is little over a century old, but in that time the proportion of natural to artificially made fibers has changed from all natural to 70% artificial.

See **Vol. I: Plastics** to find out more about the nature of plastics.

See **Vol. 3: Wood** to find out more about how paper is made from fibers.

New fibers are being constantly invented to meet new needs. For example, Kevlar® and other such materials were developed both for their fire resistance and their use as safety gloves and bulletproof vests.

When people produce artificial fibers, they are rearranging the MOLECULES of the material themselves, breaking down PETROCHEMICAL (oil-based) raw materials into building blocks, which are then re-formed into new substances with new properties. Only after they have been created do artificial fibers and filaments go through the spinning and weaving processes to make FABRICS, paper, or whatever is required.

It is important to regard natural and artificial fibers as complementary, not as competing fibers. Very often the two are used together, for each has its own unique properties. Artificial fibers dominate in the modern marketplace simply because they can be produced at a fraction of the price of natural materials and because they can be designed to meet needs that natural materials sometimes cannot. At the same time, natural materials have feel and durability that sometimes cannot be matched by artificials.

Fibers are chains of molecules

As you can see, fibers have a wide range of possible properties, which is the reason different fibers are used in different situations. Understanding their properties, making the most of them, and even improving on their properties by molecular juggling is the role of materials science.

As we said at the beginning, most fibers (except glass and some other minerals like asbestos) are chains of molecules containing carbon. The majority also contain hydrogen and oxygen.

(*Left*) This weatherproof protective clothing and the crate are made of the same material—a plastic. Both are strong and waterproof. But one is made into a sheet and so is rigid, while the other is made into a fiber and is flexible.

Many also contain nitrogen. These long chains of molecules occur whether the fiber is natural or made in a factory. The characteristics of the fiber are determined by how the atoms in the molecules and the molecules themselves join. These molecular arrangements will be covered in detail throughout this book.

All fibers and filaments, both natural and artificial, are chemicals called POLYMERS. The word polymer comes from the Greek "*poly*," meaning "many," and "*mer*," meaning "parts." This describes the way that polymers like fibers and filaments are made up of long chains of the same building block, often millions of units long.

The building block of a polymer is the molecule. Some polymers build end to end to make straight chains; others make branching chains. Sometimes branches may join and connect the polymer together. The properties of all fibers are controlled by the way the chains form and how the branches connect.

Another important thing about fibers is the size of their molecules. The bigger the molecule, the stronger the fiber, but the more sticky it is in liquid form, and the higher the temperature at which it will melt. As a result, artificial fibers are a compromise between strength and workability.

(*Above and below*) Animal hair is valuable to humans. For millennia we have used hair from animals such as sheep, goats, and llamas to produce natural fibers, which in turn we make into fabrics.

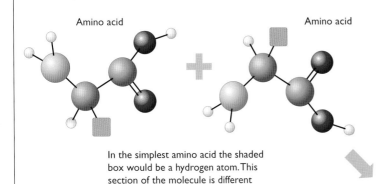

Amino acid   Amino acid

In the simplest amino acid the shaded box would be a hydrogen atom. This section of the molecule is different for different amino acids.

A section of protein chain

Water

Water is a product of this condensation polymerization process.

Natural polymers

There are two kinds of polymers that make up natural fibers. They are called animal PROTEINS (in which amino acids are joined by chemicals called amides) and plant CARBOHYDRATES (in which chains of simple sugar molecules add together).

Proteins and carbohydrates are formed in different ways. All animal silk, hair, or wool is pushed out, or extruded, from special places on the skin or special organs. Although proteins are extruded as filaments, hair often falls out when it has reached a certain length, and then a new filament begins to grow again. That is why hair (including wool) is usually put in the category of fiber.

CELLULOSE is the building block of plant cells. The cells overlap. They have a definite length and are not produced in filaments. As a plant stem grows, for example, it produces new fibers, rather than extending the existing ones.

The forces holding the molecules together are very strong and hard to break (see the manufacture of rayon on pages 12 and 39). Natural polymers usually have melting points that are so high that they decompose, or char, before they melt. This makes them very difficult to work with or to re-form into fibers with different properties.

Of the natural fibers, those with long chains and few branches are the most useful for making into fabrics. Thus cellulose is a useful fiber-former because its molecules lie in long chains with few branches. By contrast, starches, which

(*Above*) A natural animal fiber or filament is made of proteins. The building blocks of proteins are amino acids. To make a fiber such as a hair, the animal cell builds proteins using amino acids. Each time this reaction takes place, water is produced. This is a process called CONDENSATION POLYMERIZATION. Nylon and polyester are two artificial fibers that also formed by condensation polymerization (see pages 14 and 42).

(*Right*) Hemp fibers are from the stem of the hemp plant. The fibers are extracted by crushing and drying the stems, followed by shaking, which separates the woody part of the stem from the cellulose fibers. Fibers up to almost 2 meters long can be obtained. Each fiber is a single long cell, which is naturally dark brown. It cannot be bleached and so is used as a rough, strong fiber. It is used for sacking (burlap), canvas, twine, and similar purposes.

(*Above and below*) Coir is a fiber made from coconut husks. The husks are kept and dried. They are then buried in mud flats until the matrix has rotted away and left only the tough fibers. They can then be used to make hard-wearing materials such as doormats.

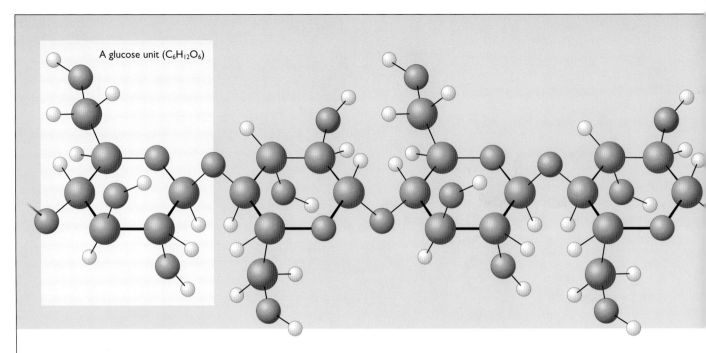

A glucose unit ($C_6H_{12}O_6$)

contain the same basic molecules, do not form useful fabric fibers because their chains are branched and coiled up, and cannot be separated.

Artificial polymers

Artificial fibers, also sometimes called man-made fibers, are fibers that have been modified in some chemical way from natural fibers or created from materials not related to natural fibers.

Natural cellulose fibers can be reconstituted to make new materials. The fiber that results is artificial in the sense that it does not occur naturally in this form. However, because the new materials still contain cellulose, they are called REGENERATED FIBERS. Rayon is the main example of this.

Synthetic fibers are polymers that do not have either natural proteins or cellulose as their starting point. They almost exclusively use products obtained from PETROLEUM. Synthetic polymers can be thought of as designer polymers.

Petroleum is a mixture of substances that readily combine into chains. Petroleum also contains a huge variety of molecules, each of different sizes, so the possibilities of producing a polymer with useful properties are good.

(*Above*) This is a rayon molecule. Like other polymers, it is made up of a string of repeating chemical units—rather like a long train in which all the carriages are alike.

Rayon is derived from cellulose (processed wood chips such as the ones below), which in turn is made up of a string of glucose units.

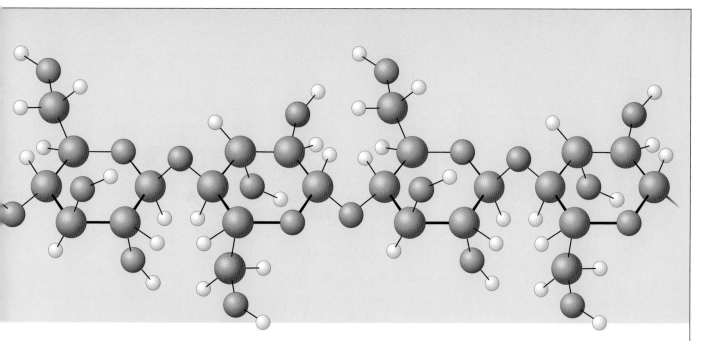

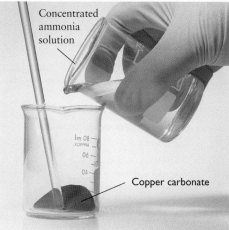

Concentrated ammonia solution

Copper carbonate

(*Below*) This simple laboratory demonstration shows how a rayon "fiber" can be generated using cellulose. The paper is the source of the cellulose.

Deep-blue-colored tetraamminecopper(II)

Filter paper

Pipette loaded with cellulose dissolved in tetraamminecopper(II) solution

Petri dish containing dilute sulfuric acid

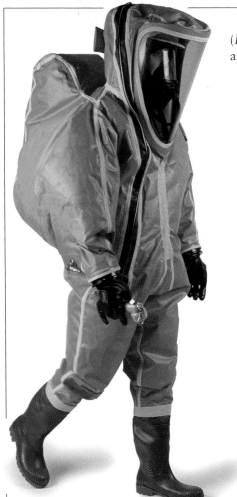

(*Left*) Synthetic polymers can be designed to have special properties such as resisting heat and burning. This is useful in such cases as firefighting.

For example, polymers can be made with lower melting points than natural polymers. As a result, they will melt before they decompose, and so they can be melted and then extruded as a filament. They can also be designed with long chains that pack together well and give the filament strength. Indeed, some polymer filaments are stronger, size for size, than steel. As a demonstration of this, bulletproof vests are made of synthetic fibers, not steel links.

How synthetic fibers are made

Synthetic fibers are made in two ways. First is a series of steps in which two molecules are made to join, then these pieces are made to join with others, and on and on. This chemical reaction is called step growth or CONDENSATION POLYMERIZATION, and it is the way nylon and polyester are made. Step growth occurs by the reaction of two chemicals.

See **Vol. 1: Plastics** *to find out more about plastics and polymerization.*

(*Below*) This is the molecule that is the basic unit of nylon. Nylon is formed by a chemical reaction between an acid and a base (see pages 32 and 33).

This represents a unit of hexamethylenediamine, or 1,6-diaminohexane ($H_2N(CH_2)_6NH_2$).

Hydrogen

Nitrogen

Carbon

Oxygen

This represents a unit of adipic acid (hexandioic acid $HOOC(CH_2)_4COOH$).

Condensation polymerization

This represents a section of the condensation polymer nylon 6,6.

Water

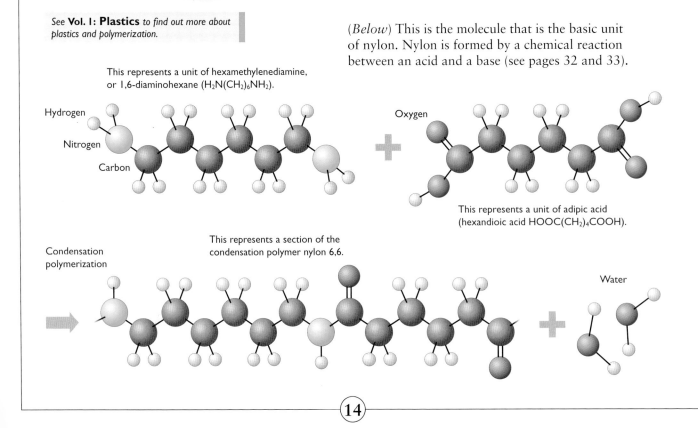

Chain growth, or ADDITION POLYMERIZATION, occurs within a single chemical when it is encouraged to link end to end with its neighbors. This process needs lots of energy and special chemicals (called CATALYSTS) to make the molecules join in straight chains without branches. As a result, the nature of the fiber produced is very sensitive to the branches that do form.

Caring for fibers in fabrics

As you have seen, fibers can come from many sources and as a result have many properties. It is not always easy to know what fibers or filaments are used just by looking at a fabric. In addition, many fabrics are made from a mixture of both natural and artificial fibers (for reasons we will discuss through the later sections of this book).

We have also seen that some fibers will char when heated, others melt. Some will let water in, and others will not. For these and a variety of other reasons we need help in deciding how to care for the fibers that we use, especially when they are made into fabrics used for shirts, skirts, trousers, and the like.

To help with this process, manufacturers use an internationally recognized system of care instructions. They are the instructions found on the inside of the garment. Following these instructions is vital because, as you have seen, inappropriate care can lead to garments being melted or charred.

(*Above and below*) If you look inside a garment, you will find instructions on caring for it. Care is vital to make sure harm does not come to the most vulnerable of the fibers.

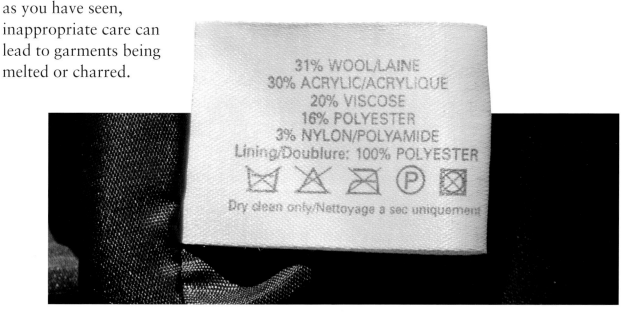

31% WOOL/LAINE
30% ACRYLIC/ACRYLIQUE
20% VISCOSE
16% POLYESTER
3% NYLON/POLYAMIDE
Lining/Doublure: 100% POLYESTER

Dry clean only/Nettoyage a sec uniquement

Ironing, permanent, and durable-press finishing

Many fibers resist changes of shape when dry but shrink and lose their straightness when wet. That is why washed materials often shrink, and why they dry to a creased finish. Sometimes the pleats and other features carefully put into new clothing will drop out on washing.

All of these changes are problems. There are two ways to overcome them. Fibers are quite difficult to change when they are cool, but at a particular temperature they will change shape quite easily. Getting to a temperature high enough is the purpose of ironing. Each fiber has its own temperature, which is why an iron has many temperature settings.

Ironing is a temporary way of improving the finish of a fabric. There are more permanent ways of getting a finish. The finish can be put into the fabric at a high melting point. Just as there is a temperature for ironing, there is also a temperature at which some artificial fibers can be changed permanently. To be useful, it has to be applied to fibers that can be heated way above normal washing and ironing temperatures yet still not melt or

(*Above and below*) Ironing is important, but it only works until the fabric becomes moist again. This often happens unnoticed when sweat soaks into the fabric.

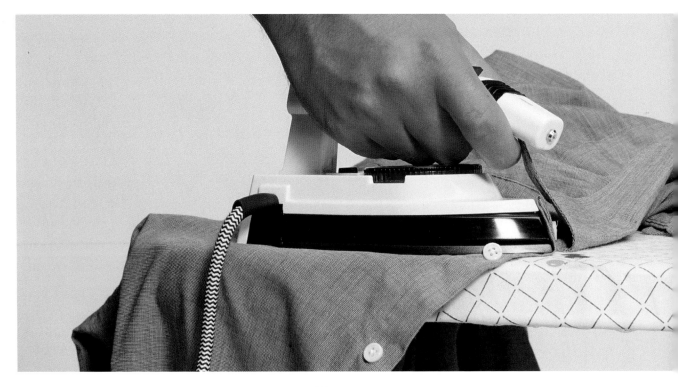

char. Polyester, the most commonly used artificial fiber, is one of them.

At this high temperature (called the tensile glass temperature) the fibers can be changed permanently from a rigid, glasslike form to a plastic one. This is the temperature at which permanent-press features can be added to a fabric. These features will remain in the fabric no matter how many times it is washed and ironed.

Another approach is a chemical treatment, often called durable press. Many fibers are partly held together by special bonds called hydrogen bonds, which link the chains of molecules in a polymer (a process called cross linking). This makes the fibers very stable and resistant to change. That is why it is difficult to wrinkle a dry fabric.

However, hydrogen bonds are the same bonds that hold water molecules together, so in damp conditions (for example, when wearing sweaty clothes) water molecules can also be bonded by the hydrogen bonds. Water then begins to get trapped and bonded between the chains. This breaks up the tightly cross-linked structure of the dry material. In fact, technically, water acts as a PLASTICIZER, making it easier for the chains to take on a new shape. If the fabric now becomes creased, such as happens when wearing clothes or washing them, there are fewer hydrogen bonds to keep the chains held tightly in shape.

If a fabric like this is to resist creasing, then new bonds have to be provided that are not affected by water. This is the basis of easy-care and permanent-press treatments of fabrics. It is usually achieved by dipping the fabric in formaldehyde. Formaldehyde is not soluble in water. The formaldehyde produces its own bonds between chains.

If the crease-resistant process is to be used, then any desired pleats have to be put in place before the treatment.

Using formaldehyde can make the fabric wear out more quickly. To compensate for this problem, fibers are blended. Some of the fibers then take on the crease-resisting chemical, while others in the blend do not, so keeping their strength. For this reason polyester fibers are often blended with cotton or rayon. The polyester fibers provide the easy-care finish, and the rayon or cotton add strength or wear-resistance.

Microfibers

You have already seen that fiber sizes vary enormously. In fact, that has a large influence on how fibers behave, for example, in how waterproof they are and how easily they breathe (let water vapor through).

Some new synthetic fibers are made with a very small diameter. The fiber, when woven, is still open enough to allow moisture to flow through, but it is fine enough to prevent water getting through. Previously this could only be achieved by using special chemical treatments, for example, by coating the fabric with silicone.

There is clearly much more development possible in fiber technology, and in time it may allow fiber manufacture to overcome a whole raft of limitations that are still present in many fibers (see page 46).

(*Left and below*) Some synthetic fibers, such as polyester, have a natural resistance to being made wet. That makes them suitable rainproof materials. But the waterproof qualities of polyester are still not sufficient to keep water out because the water gets between the fibers. The traditional way to make a material waterproof is to treat it with a water-repellent chemical.

However, by making the material with microfibers, that is, fibers with an incredibly fine diameter, the finer mesh of the fabric also makes it less likely that water can pass through. In this case the material is naturally rain-resistant and does not need special surface treatment to repel water. Surface treatments on outdoor garments can make them less able to breathe because the pores become clogged. They also tend to wear off in time. As a result, the use of microfibers in these circumstances would make a garment more comfortable and waterproof for the length of its life.

Microfibers have the additional advantage that they keep the wind out, making the fiber better for preventing body heat loss.

Fabrics of microfibers keep out the wind.

Microfibers keep out the rain without surface treatments.

Microfibers still allow water vapor to pass through.

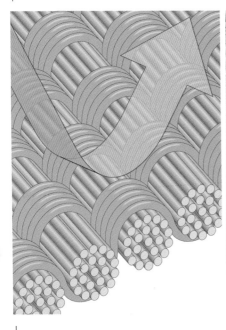

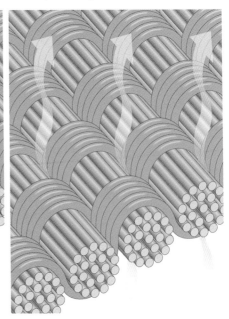

2: Natural fibers

Natural fibers may be solid (if they grow from the skin of an animal), or they may be long tubelike cells (if from a plant). Natural fibers are turned into fabrics or made into paper.

There are many natural fibers, including silk, cotton, hemp, jute, raffia, and wool, but only a few have suitable strength, flexibility, resistance to wear, and other properties to make them useful to people.

Leaf fiber

Leaf fiber comes from flowering plants with parallel-veined leaves such as grasses and palms. Commonly used leaf fibers include hemp and sisal. The agave family of plants has long, sword-shaped leaves, which have fiber bundles many tens of centimeters long. They are used by the plant to strengthen the leaf. The fibers are made of many overlapping cells stuck together with natural gums.

The fibers from leaves are usually hard, stiff, and coarse. It is usually not worthwhile trying to separate out the fibers, and they are kept as natural fiber bundles and sold for cord and rope. Sisal is the most important such crop.

All leaf plants are difficult and expensive to harvest and of low value when put on the market. As a result, they are open to competition from artificial fibers.

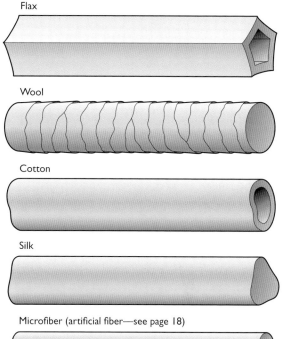

Flax

Wool

Cotton

Silk

Microfiber (artificial fiber—see page 18)

(*Above*) Natural fibers have a variety of shapes.

(*Right*) Sisal is a coarse, tough leaf fiber. It is not comfortable but good for scraping when knitted into a mit such as this scouring glove.

Boll fiber

The fibers from seed cases, or BOLLS, of plants are the finest in a plant. They are also free from the many impurities found in leaf and stem fibers. Boll fibers include kapok and cotton. They are made of single long cells and are not stuck together with natural gums.

Boll fibers are among the most valuable of fibers for high-quality fabrics. They are also used in some high-quality papers.

Bast fiber

The fibers of the stems of plants—called BAST FIBERS—are the most widely used plant fibers. They are softer and more flexible fibers than leaf fibers, although not as fine as boll fibers.

The plants most widely used for their stem fibers are those flowering plants with net-veined leaves. The most important fibers from this group are flax, hemp, and jute.

The fibers can be meters long and made of overlapping cells bound into bundles by natural GUM. The fibers are found between the bark and the woody core of the plant.

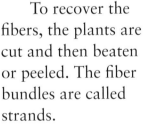

(*Above and below*) Cotton is the fiber enclosing the cotton seed. The pod containing the cotton filaments and seeds is called a cotton boll.

To recover the fibers, the plants are cut and then beaten or peeled. The fiber bundles are called strands.

Bast fibers are strong and more pliable than leaf strands and so are preferred for ropes, coarser sacks, and some heavy-duty fabrics. Flax is the raw material for linen.

How natural fibers have been used

Fibers have been used for many thousands of years. First came the use of cultivated plant fibers such as hemp. Flax (for making linen), wool, silk, and cotton fabrics also date back to ancient times.

Many natural fibers begin as an unpromising collection of short threads, or STAPLE. The challenge facing people thousands of years ago was how to turn them into something useful.

People must have noticed how natural fibers tend to get TANGLED, or MATTED, easily. Their natural curl and often scaly surfaces make it easy for them to intertwine and hold fast.

When you try to pull out matted hairs, they naturally start to pull together into a strand. That is, the scales and curl in the hairs mechanically fasten the hairs together. Pulling them tends to pull the strands in the same direction, so they fit together better. That is why a strand is formed.

Pulling out matted hair in this fashion is a crude form of spinning. In the actual spinning process the short fibers are teased out and at the same time are brought together under tension and given a twist. The tension and twist help compact the fibers and make them lock together even better. Spinning bobbins and spinning wheels are simple machines designed to produce the tension and twist.

(Above and below) Hemp is made into sacking and is also used for webbing in upholstery.

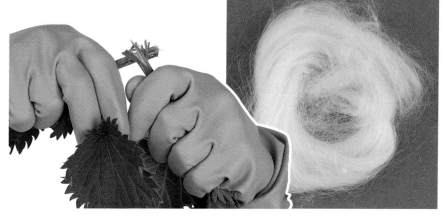

(Right) The fibers that make up the stem of this nettle plant are clear to see if it is snapped. The fine white fibers have been extracted from a nettle plant.

When the fibers have been pulled into line and twisted, they make a bundle of fibers called a YARN. The word "yarn" applies to any spun fiber, wool, cotton, and so on, for example, knitting yarn. Some yarns have special names, for example, thread, twine, and rope.

(*Left and below*) This is a simple form of spinning by hand. The weighted spindle is given a twist, and it pulls the fibers together and winds them in one step.

(*Left*) Each of the separate strands that you can see in the skein of gray wool is a yarn.

Spinning is a mechanical process. It uses the natural tendency that hairs have to cling together to turn short fibers into longer fibers that can be made into fabrics. But because that is all that has happened, the fibers can be pulled apart. That is how spun material breaks. The fibers do not usually break so much as pull apart.

Spun material is useful for ropes, but it becomes far more useful when it is made into a form of net. That turns a yarn into a fabric. The process of making a net of this kind is called weaving.

Weaving and related types of net-making such as knitting take two sets of yarns and pass them under and over one another so that they are held in place. This process also makes the tearing of the spun yarn less likely because it helps spread out forces across the whole fabric.

For most of their long history fibers have been spun (made into a long yarn) and woven (made into a fabric) by hand. It was a time-consuming business. The Industrial Revolution changed this by mechanizing many of the straightforward textile processes.

(*Right*) This is simple weaving to make bags using sisal string.

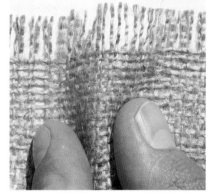

(*Left*) This is a fabric—a mesh of interwoven fibers in sheet form.

(*Above and below*) The most common way of converting yarn into fabric is weaving. Normally the yarn is interwoven on a loom using a warp (that runs lengthwise) and a weft (running widthwise). Weaving by this method goes back as far as 6,000 years ago.

(*Above and below*) Knitting is another method for making fabrics and works by interlocking loops of yarn. It is a highly regarded craft but is done industrially using knitting machines.

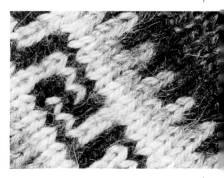

In the 19th century, and especially in the 20th century, natural fibers were challenged for the first time by artificial fibers. The first artificial fibers were reconstituted natural fibers such as rayon. But soon after, completely new, or synthetic, fibers were invented. This has changed the balance of fiber use in favor of synthetic, while intense competition has caused prices to fall. Textiles are now cheap enough to be worn for a while as a fashion item and then thrown out, something that just half a century ago would have been unthinkable.

Properties of natural fibers

Many natural fibers absorb water and swell. That is an important property for their use in fabrics. For example, it allows fibers to soak up water-based dyes.

Natural fibers do not change significantly when heated. That is very different from artificial fibers, which soften as they become hot. No natural fibers melt. Instead, they DECOMPOSE, or char, at high temperatures.

Once a natural fiber has stopped being part of living tissue, it tends to turn yellow if exposed to sunlight or heat (as for example with straw and paper). When natural fibers age in this way, they also become weaker.

Because natural fibers are made by living things, they are part of the cycle of life. This means that natural fibers are food for decomposers such as bacteria and fungi. They are also food for a wide range of insects, of which clothes moths and carpet beetles are perhaps the best known to most people.

(*Above and below*) It is not always easy to tell which fiber has been used in a garment. But it will always be stated on the label.

(*Above*) Cotton was a favored material for early settlers because it kept them cool in summer when they still had hard work to do. We still use cotton for its cool, fresh feel.

Cotton

(*Below*) A selection of dyed cotton threads.

Cotton

Cotton is a subtropical shrublike plant with white flowers. As the seeds mature, they become surrounded by a mass of fine, soft seed hairs or fibers. The whole seed pod is called a cotton boll. The cotton is harvested when the boll bursts, for it is then that the cotton fiber is easiest to collect. The seeds are separated from the fibers by a mechanical combing process called ginning.

The fibers range from 1 to 6 cm long and contain 90% cellulose. This length is called the staple length. The cotton is collected and bound up in a bale.

It is hardest to cultivate plants with a long staple length. They are mainly Egyptian and Sea Island (near Florida, South Carolina, and Georgia) cottons, and their staple length is from 3 to 6 cm. They make the most expensive fabrics. More plentiful is the cotton with less than 3 cm staple length, such as is mainly grown in mainland America. These cottons are used as blends with other fibers and for carpets and blankets.

The cotton is processed by removing any impurities such as soil by combing and getting the fibers to line up in a process called carding. The fibers are then drawn together and spun into a yarn and wound onto a bobbin.

The spun yarn can be woven in the same way as other fabrics.

Cotton fabrics last well because they resist rubbing. Cotton will also accept many dyes. It is comfortable to wear because it acts like a natural wick, soaking up body moisture and releasing it to the air.

(*Left and below*) Cutting a fleece. The shearer's hand is covered in the natural lanolin that makes the fleece water-resistant.

Wool

Wool is an animal fiber like the protective hairy coating on most other animals. The fiber covering is called the fleece. Sheep, goats, and camels all develop wool.

In sheep the natural outer and coarser hairs that were once a feature of wild sheep have been bred out, so the downy undercoat now makes up almost all of the fleece. As a result, sheep are more productive of wool than, for example, Kashmir goats.

Wool is obtained by shearing the sheep to leave the fleece in one piece. The fleece contains a natural waterproofing grease called lanolin, which, once removed, can be used as a base for many cosmetics.

Wool is made of a protein called keratin. The wool fibers are coarser than many other animal fibers and most

Wool

(*Left and right*) Wool is used in sweaters, rugs, and carpets. It has a better feel than many synthetics and can be harder wearing. However, it tends to be expensive, is harder to wash, and is subject to attack by moths.

plant fibers. They are made of overlapping scales. Most wool diameters are between 16 to 40 microns (millionths of a meter) and up to 20 cm long. Longer fibers are used for fabrics called worsteds and for suits and other smoother fabrics; shorter fibers are used for tweeds and other coarser fabrics. Natural wool ranges in color from white to gray and brown and black.

Wool has good resistance to breaking but is weaker when wet than when dry. Once pulled out of shape, wool will spring back to its original length. This helps the fabric retain its shape during washing and helps in its crease resistance.

Wool also has a natural waviness, or CRIMP. This means that the fibers interlock easily and leave natural gaps that trap air. That helps the wool appear soft, while the trapped air acts as an insulator and helps the wool feel warm. Wool has quite a low density, so that it can be made into lightweight products. Wool is also easily dyed.

Wool acts as a natural moisture absorber and wick, soaking up moisture from the body and transferring it to the air. Moisture is absorbed and

(*Below left*) Cashmere is the very fine fiber from the goats that live in the Kashmir Himalayas of Asia.

The hair used to make shawls and other garments is the fine undercoat beneath the coarse wool. It is combed out during the molting season. The fibers it yields are between 3 and 10 cm long. The amounts of this undercoat are small, and one pullover needs the product of about five goats. The hair has scales like that of wool, but finer. The fibers are also finer than any wool, averaging about 15 micrometers in diameter. The most common color is gray, but hairs can be white, black, and brown.

It is not as strong a fiber as wool, nor does it have the durability of wool. It is therefore exclusively a fashion item.

given out slowly, so although wool is slow to feel damp, it is also slow to dry out. On the other hand, slow drying means that woollen garments when worn wet do not cause chilling to the skin, as would be the case for quick-drying materials such as cotton.

Wool can be stretched during manufacture and hold this longer shape. However, when washed, it shrinks back to its original length. That is why woollens tend to shrink on first washing. Wool is easily harmed by high-temperature washing and is food for certain moths. It is not very resistant to mildew.

The natural matting of wool, so carefully avoided during clothes washing, can be encouraged in a process called felting. Felt is used for pool tables, tennis balls, felt-tipped pens, and hats.

(*Left*) Felt still has a range of special uses, including hats and felt-tipped pens.

Silk

Silk is a filament from cocoons produced by the caterpillars known as silkworms.

Silkworms raised by people are allowed to go through their larval stage (silkworm) and then pupate (create a cocoon for themselves by spinning a silk thread). The silk they release is a continuous filament. Two filaments are produced, each of a protein called fibrin. The silkworm also puts out a glue called sericin, which binds the filaments together.

In the natural life cycle of the silkworm the adult moth emerges by breaking open the cocoon. People don't want this since it breaks the filament, and so the pupae are killed inside their cocoons using steam.

The cocoon is placed in hot water, which softens the glue and allows the filament to be unwound. A single cocoon can produce a continuous filament nearly a kilometer long.

Several cocoons are unwound at the same time, making a twisted strand of raw silk. Strands are combined until a yarn of usable thickness is produced.

(*Above and above right*) Silk moth cocoons are placed in tubs of hot water to soften the gluelike substance that covers the silk filaments. The filaments can then be drawn off to make threads.

At this stage the natural glue is dissolved away by boiling the fibers in a soap solution.

Once the silk has been cleaned, it is soft. This silk is also shiny—a property that comes from the flat faces of the triangular section of the filaments. The thickness of the yarn is measured in a scale called denier, which is a scale based on the weight in grams of 9,000 m of silk.

Special treatments are sometimes applied to give the silk a rustling sound when it is made into clothing.

Silk can absorb up to a third of its weight in moisture before it feels damp. It is easy to dye and does not easily rot.

Silk

(*Right and below*) Silk is expensive and so is used in special products such as wedding dresses, silk flowers, and ties.

Dyeing natural fibers

Dyeing is different for natural and for artificial fibers. Dyes are held on the surface of natural fibers. A spun fiber may be made of hundreds of strands, but within these strands can be tens of millions of tiny spaces called pores. They dramatically increase the surface area onto which a dye can hold. As a result of these pores, cotton and wool have real surface areas of 45,000 square meters per kilogram.

When a color is applied to this kind of fiber, it is necessary to build up a layer of dye molecules up to ten thousand molecules thick. The thickness of dyes is trapped and stored in the pores rather than on the fiber surfaces. That is the reason the color is not easily rubbed off during use.

Modern dyes—called reactive dyes—are designed so that the dye molecules also fix themselves into the pores by bonding with molecules on the surface of the pores. Older dyes simply rely on being trapped in the pores.

Most dyeing of natural fibers can be done simply by dipping the fiber in the dye solution. This is called direct dyeing. However, many fibers do not absorb dyes well, and some intermediate chemical, called a mordant, is needed to fasten the dyes to the fiber.

A common mordant is alum (potassium aluminum sulfate). The fibers are first dipped in the mordant, and the potassium and aluminum in the mordant fix themselves onto the fiber. When the dye is applied in a separate dipping, the dyes are attracted to the potassium and aluminum on the fabric surface. This makes a soluble dye insoluble, so that the dye will not be removed when the fabric is washed.

See **Vol. 6: Dyes, paints, and adhesives** to find out more about dyeing.

(*Right*) Naturally dyed fibers hanging out to dry.

3: Artificial fibers

Artificial fibers, also called man-made fibers, are fibers manufactured from a raw material. As mentioned in the first section, there are two kinds of artificial fibers: REGENERATED FIBERS and synthetic fibers. During processing, the raw material of an artificial fiber is separated into simple molecules, which are then made to join into new polymers.

Regenerated fibers use the same chemicals that make up natural fibers. For example, rayon uses the same cellulose as is found in wood. The raw material for rayon is a liquid containing cellulose that is produced as part of wood pulp processing.

Synthetic fibers are those in which the fibers are manufactured from a material that was not originally similar to that of natural fibers. Polyester and nylon are examples of synthetic fibers. Nearly all synthetic fibers begin as petroleum, although natural gas and coal are also used. Synthetic fibers are made in far bigger quantities and used for a much greater range of fibers than regenerated fibers.

(*Above and below*) The raw materials of artificial fibers begin as a collection of liquids and gases distilled from petroleum.

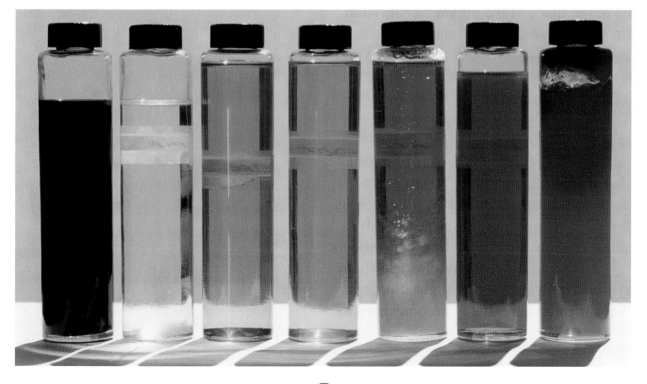

There is little or no difference between the chemistry of the materials used to make synthetic fibers and those used to make any kind of plastic. It is simply that in the case of synthetic fibers, the molecules are made into long, flexible strands without interlinked branches.

Once made into fiber, synthetics can be used in the same way as natural fibers. The big advantage of many synthetic fibers is that they resist the rotting and attack by insects that beset natural fibers. They can also be designed to have particular characteristics.

Polyester or polyethylene terephthalate (PET, PETE) are now the main synthetic fibers, accounting for more than half of worldwide production.

Characteristics of artificial fibers

All artificial fibers are polymers. The differences between the many kinds of fibers lie in the shape of the polymer chains and the materials from which they are made. For example, some chains remain long and straight, while others develop branches along their length.

Many polymers are unsuitable for making into fibers because they develop interlinked branching networks of molecules that stop them from being strong when made into fibers. That is why, for example, no fibers are made of polystyrene. Only single chain polymers can be used for fibers.

An important property of single-chain synthetic polymers is that on heating, they will soften and eventually become molten.

See **Vol. I: Plastics** to find out more about the chemistry of plastics.

(*Below*) Synthetic fibers such as nylon can be made in a beaker in the laboratory using two chemicals. Hexanedioyl chloride is poured carefully onto hexamethylenediamine. The chemicals react across the surface where they touch. The white precipitate is the nylon forming.

(*Right*) The nylon has to be carefully teased from the liquids at a constant rate to produce a filament. Of course, this process can only continue while enough of the chemicals remain to react. This is called batch processing. For industrial use a more continuous way of producing a filament is used. Solid nylon pellets are melted and then extruded through a spinneret to produce a controlled filament (see page 35).

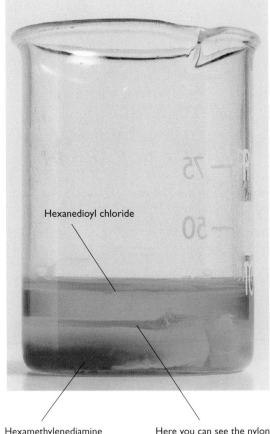

Hexanedioyl chloride

Hexamethylenediamine dissolved in water

Here you can see the nylon forming at the interface between the two liquids.

Nylon "thread" is pulled through the upper liquid.

Branched chain polymers will not soften or melt at all without decomposing (They are the ones that char when too hot an iron is applied to them.) Acrylics are an example. In this case the polymer cannot be melted in order to spin it. Instead, it must be dissolved and then spun from a solution.

Both kinds of polymer can be made into liquids that can be extruded through fine holes to form filaments. This makes them very suitable for mass production.

Furthermore, these long chains have great strength, so that they will not break easily even when formed into thin fibers.

Not all long-chain polymers make useful fibers. That is because the fibers have to have quite high melting points; otherwise they will melt when they are ironed. At the other end of the scale, if the melting point is too high, it will be hard to melt the polymer in the factory in order to spin it.

The differences in temperature can be quite critical, as anyone who has ironed a synthetic fabric at too high an iron setting will know to their cost. Polypropylene, for example, has a melting temperature of 176°C. It is used as fibers in clothing, upholstery, and carpet fabrics. A closely related polymer, polyethylene, however, has a lower melting temperature at 137°C, too low for use in most domestic fabrics.

Polyesters are a group of easily made and cheap synthetic fibers. Terylene® is an example. It has a higher melting point (265°C) than polypropylene but is still easy to work with. Nylon also has a melting point of 265°C, again, making it easy to work with and spin from molten form.

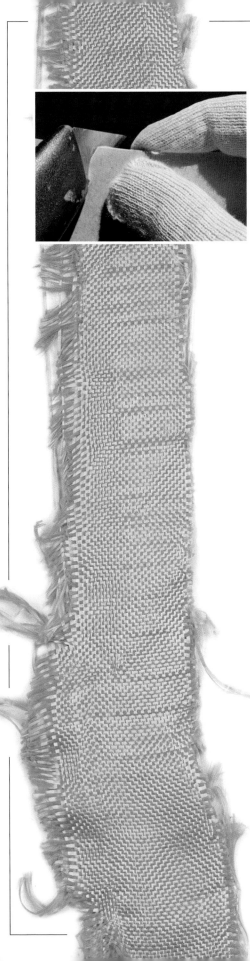

(*Left*) This is a strip of Kevlar.

(*Right*) The manufacture of nylon uses melt spinning. Nylon pellets are heated to 265°C to form a molten polymer solution. This molten solution is forced—extruded—through tiny holes in a spinneret. The solid filaments of nylon produced are treated in a cooling bath and spun into a long yarn of thread and wound onto a reel. Polyester fiber is produced using a similar melt spinning process.

In a few cases very high melting point polymers can have advantages that outweigh their difficulty in manufacture. That is the case with the ring-shaped molecules that are made into materials known under such trade names as Kevlar®. They are used as fire-resistant and bulletproof fabrics as well as stiffening materials in boats and aircraft.

Spinning

The most common way of producing fibers from artificial polymers is to force them in liquid form through the small holes of a metal object that works rather like a showerhead and is known as a SPINNERET. This is a process of extrusion, and it produces a continuous fiber, or filament.

Liquids are a form of matter in which the molecules can slip easily past one another and so can readily take on new shapes. In an artificial fiber factory this process is known as spinning. However, it is not at all like the process of spinning natural fibers, in which many short fibers are twisted together to make a yarn.

There are four methods of spinning filaments from manufactured fibers: wet, dry, melt, and gel spinning. More than one process can be used for many polymers. In wet and dry spinning the polymer is dissolved in a liquid solvent, so the solvent has to be removed as soon as it passes through the spinneret. How this is done depends on the solvent. In some cases the solvent has to be reacted with another chemical in order to precipitate the polymer. This is

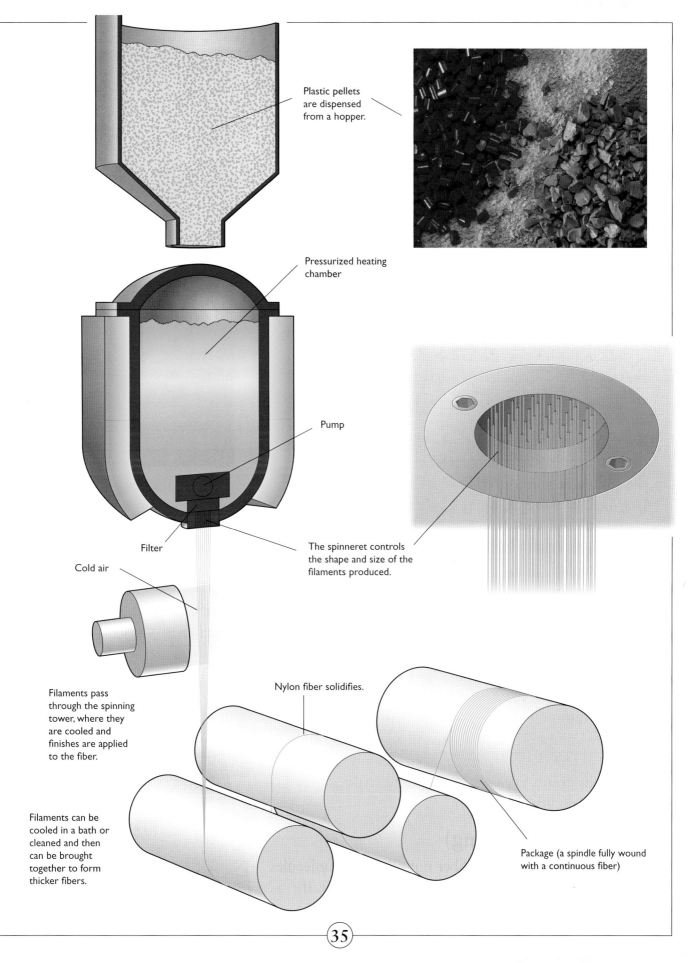

Plastic pellets are dispensed from a hopper.

Pressurized heating chamber

Pump

Filter

The spinneret controls the shape and size of the filaments produced.

Cold air

Filaments pass through the spinning tower, where they are cooled and finishes are applied to the fiber.

Filaments can be cooled in a bath or cleaned and then can be brought together to form thicker fibers.

Nylon fiber solidifies.

Package (a spindle fully wound with a continuous fiber)

called wet spinning. In other cases the solvent can be made to evaporate without the use of any other chemical. This is called dry spinning.

Wet spinning is the oldest process and is still commonly used (see the viscose process on page 40). In this case fibers emerge from the spinneret into a chemical bath where the filaments are made to solidify by chemical reaction. Acrylic, rayon, aramid, and modacrylic can be produced this way.

Dry spinning is now used for making specialty fibers such as acetate, triacetate, acrylic, and spandex.

In some cases no solvent is needed at all. This is the case with melt and gel spinning.

The most economical method of spinning is melt spinning. In this case the polymer is heated until it melts and then extruded through the spinneret. It is solidified by cooling. Nylon, olefin, and polyester are often produced this way.

One important property of melt spinning is that the melt-spun fibers can be extruded from the spinneret with different cross-sectional shapes (for example, round, square, trilobal, pentagonal, octagonal, and hollow). These shapes can be used to give important extra characteristics to the fiber. For example, trilobal-shaped fibers reflect more light and give an attractive sparkle to textiles; pentagonal-shaped fibers reflect the light less and do not show dirt as much as other fibers. Octagonal-shaped fibers reflect the light very little. Hollow fibers trap air and so have insulating properties. They make hollow-fill materials used in outdoor garments.

Gel spinning uses a gel for extrusion. A gel is neither a solid nor a liquid, but consists of liquid crystals. Here the polymer chains are bound together at various points even while they are extruded. This can add strength to the fiber.

Stretching (drawing)

In a newly spun synthetic fiber not all of the molecules are in long, straight threads parallel to the fiber. If

(*Above*) Polyester can be manufactured in a wide variety of forms, including this one, which has a metallic look.

See **Vol. 6: Dyes, paints, and adhesives** to find out more about the dyeing process.

they can all be lined up and brought close together, they will be much stronger. So, after the fiber has been spun, it is often pulled, or drawn. This causes the molecules in it to line up and move closer. Some fibers become several times their spun length during this process. Once they have all closed up, the fiber will not draw out any further. Fiber for tire cord is made this way.

Giving a synthetic fiber a texture

Synthetic fibers are long filaments. But they can be given quite different feels by processing further. For example, a fiber that will be spun into yarn and used as a substitute for wool needs to look as wavy as wool. This waviness is called CRIMPING. Crimping is produced by passing the fiber through intermeshing wheels like gear wheels. Crimping can also be produced during spinning by extruding together two different polymers so they join as they leave the spinneret and before they solidify. Then, when the fiber is drawn, one polymer will pull out more than the one it is joined to, and this will make the fiber form into a spiral.

Yet another way is to twist two fibers together as they come from the spinneret, wait for them to cool so the twist is set in the fiber, then untwist them.

Dyeing artificial fibers

For natural fibers the dyeing process is all very straightforward. However, synthetic fibers tend to be more difficult to dye with natural dyes than natural fibers because they naturally repel water. This is especially the case with rayon, PET, and acrylics.

(*Left*) Fibers are widely used in tire manufacture to support the rubber and help give the tire its strength. Different fibers are used in the tread (where considerable elasticity is needed) and in the walls (where the amount of elasticity required is much smaller). Rayon and nylon are common tire fibers.

(*Above and below*) Synthetic dyes used with synthetic fibers tend to be best in outdoor conditions, retaining their strength of color much longer than natural materials.

To overcome this problem, the dyes have to be transferred using a nonwater-based solvent such as benzyl alcohol.

There are no pores in synthetic fibers, so the dye has to be deposited on the surface. One way is to dip the yarn in a hot liquid, so the fibers relax and let in some liquid and its dye, then cool the fabric so that the fibers close again.

Azo dyes are widely used with synthetic fibers. They are entirely synthetic and are based on coal and oil. The first azo dye was called aniline, and toward the end of the 19th century it revolutionized the dyeing process. The dye can actually be made while the fabric is being dyed. The dye does not necessarily have to be made up beforehand. Dyeing in this way is a two-stage process. First, one solution, called the coupler, is used. Then the fabric is dipped in a solution of an azo salt. The coupler and azo salt react on the surface of the fabric to produce a color. This is called ingrain dyeing.

Although the techniques are slightly different, in the majority of cases the fibers are dyed after they have been made, just as would happen with natural fibers. This means that a large bulk of neutral color polymer can be produced.

Some synthetics simply will not take up any kind of dye. In this case color is added to the polymer while it is being made and before it is extruded. Acrylic fibers and polypropylene fibers are of this kind. In these cases the coloring material is usually a pigment, that is, a solid material with color. Adding pigments during fiber-making also helps resist change due to light, something that is very desirable if the fabric is to be used permanently outdoors.

(*Right*) Cellulose is from processed wood chips.

Rayon fiber

Cellulose is so useful because it belongs to a large family of related chemicals called alcohols. This means that it is possible to make a variety of related, but subtly different, material easily from the same basic unit. However, cellulose chains are normally strongly held together by special bonds called hydrogen bonds. These bonds mean that cellulose cannot melt (it chars when heated) or be dissolved in common solvents.

Rayon is the most common form of artificial fiber made from dissolved cellulose (see page 12 for a representation of a rayon polymer chain). The process by which the cellulose is dissolved is called the viscose process, so much rayon is known as viscose.

To make viscose, cellulose fiber is put in a bath of caustic soda (sodium hydroxide). This produces a reaction that creates a substance called soda cellulose. The soda cellulose is squeezed to remove excess caustic soda solution, and then the soda cellulose is shredded to increase its surface area and improve the rate of chemical reaction. The soda cellulose is then allowed to stand in air. The reaction of soda cellulose with oxygen in the air is called aging.

At an appropriate moment the aged soda cellulose is put in a vat and reacted with carbon disulfide gas to form substances called xanthate ester compounds. These compounds are again dissolved in caustic soda solution, and that is when the cellulose chains pull apart, and the cellulose goes into solution.

Because the cellulose xanthate solution is very sticky, or viscous like syrup, the product was named viscose.

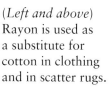

(*Left and above*) Rayon is used as a substitute for cotton in clothing and in scatter rugs.

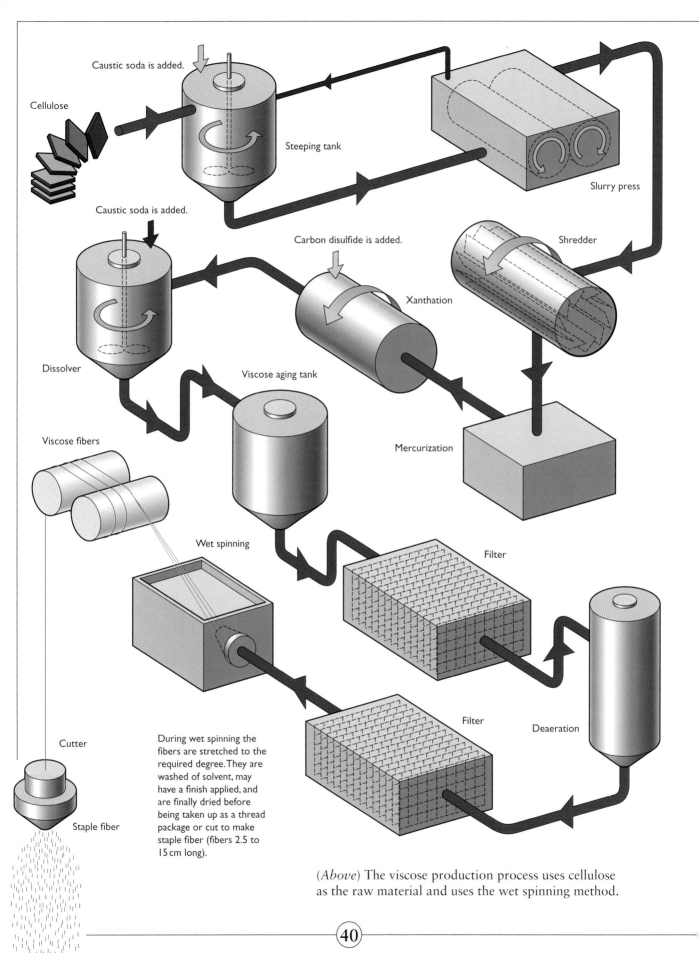

Caustic soda is added.

Cellulose

Steeping tank

Slurry press

Caustic soda is added.

Carbon disulfide is added.

Shredder

Xanthation

Dissolver

Viscose aging tank

Mercurization

Viscose fibers

Wet spinning

Filter

Cutter

During wet spinning the fibers are stretched to the required degree. They are washed of solvent, may have a finish applied, and are finally dried before being taken up as a thread package or cut to make staple fiber (fibers 2.5 to 15 cm long).

Filter

Deaeration

Staple fiber

(*Above*) The viscose production process uses cellulose as the raw material and uses the wet spinning method.

(*Above*) These shiny threads are 100% viscose.

(*Below*) This piece of lace is 75% nylon and 25% viscose. The nylon adds extra strength.

The viscose is filtered to remove undissolved materials and is then forced through a spinneret into a bath of sulfuric acid, sodium sulfate, and zinc. Complex reactions occur during which the cellulose turns into a solid filament.

Viscose is the most widely used form of rayon. Its use has declined somewhat due to environmental concerns about the release of the toxic gas carbon disulfide, which is used in its manufacture.

Viscose can feel like cotton and can be made to seem like silk. It is soft, comfortable, and easy to dye. It is often used blended with cotton to reduce cost. It is used in clothing, for bedspreads and blankets, drapes, and upholstery.

Rayon products are often unsuited to water washing and so have to be DRY CLEANED. Rayon will not stand up to high temperatures and can only be pressed with a cool iron.

High-strength rayon, produced by drawing the rayon during spinning, is used as tire cord in car tires. Rayon is also used with wood pulp for high-quality paper.

Polyester fiber

Polyester makes up over half of all man-made fiber production. Its most common form is called PET or PETE (polyethylene terephthalate). A considerable amount of polyester fiber is produced by recycling PET soft drink bottles and thus saving on petroleum supplies and avoiding landfill problems.

PET is made by reacting the chemical ethylene glycol with terephthalic acid. A special chemical called a catalyst is also needed to help form the polymer. The reaction is carried out at high temperature and in a vacuum. PET is melted and then extruded through a spinneret.

Polyester is so widely used because it is strong, it does not change shape or shrink when washed, and it is easily washed and quick drying. It also does not change its texture when wet, does not easily crease, does not rot, and can be permanently pressed.

Polyester does not, however, absorb water, and so it cannot be dyed with water-based natural dyes.

(*Left*) A colorful polyester fiber bobbin used in sewing. Common or trade names for polyester fibers include Dacron®, Terylene®, and Trevira®.

(*Below*) A polyester can be produced from a reaction between a dicarboxylic acid and a glycol or dialcohol. The product is a condensation polymer.

In the example below, terephthalic acid reacts with ethylene glycol to produce a polyester with the trade name Dacron®.

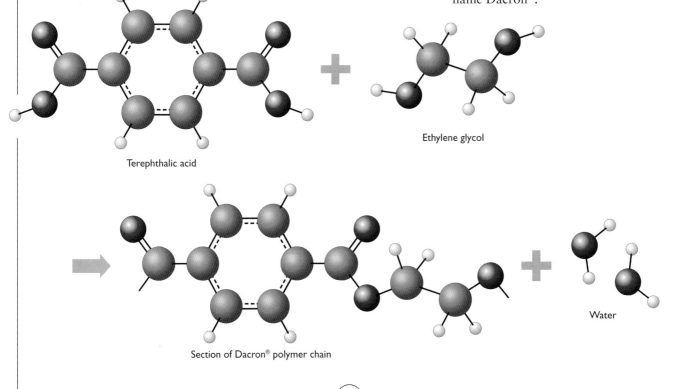

Terephthalic acid

Ethylene glycol

Water

Section of Dacron® polymer chain

(*Below*) Polyester is frequently used in sailmaking because it resists atmospheric weathering.

(*Above*) Polyester is among the most widely used artificial polymers. It is found in sports clothing as well as in everyday wear.

(*Above*) Cotton and polyester are a common mixture of cheapness and strength, as used for the binding on this book!

(*Above*) Polyester is often used as a filler for inexpensive quilts and outdoor clothing.

(*Below*) Polyester is often used to make carpet pile. It tends to produce a rather harsh and shiny finish. Better carpets are a blend of polyester and other materials such as wool.

Almost all kinds of clothing are made with polyester. It is also used in drapes, upholstery, carpets, bed linen, for ropes and nets, for thread, for tire cord, for sails, and as fiberfill for thermal clothing, pillows, and furniture.

Polyester molecules are regular and straight, so the chains link together well. However, they can still melt. Polyester is THERMOPLASTIC material, unlike many plastics whose chains prevent this, and so they decompose or char (they are THERMOSETTING plastics). Polyester can therefore be melted and re-formed, perhaps as transparent bottles or as more fibers.

Polyester has a high enough melting point to be untroubled by washing and warm (not hot) ironing. This is also important because it allows it to take a permanent-press finish. That is because, in order to remain in the shape made during manufacture, the fiber must not be reheated to a temperature called its "glass transition temperature." Below this temperature the polyester will not change shape, but above this critical point it is easy to reshape. So polyester can be made into the desired fabric at a high temperature that is still below the melting point, but the pleats or other finish will not come out during normal washing, ironing, and drying temperatures because they do not reach the glass transition temperature.

(*Right*) Acrylic is used as a substitute for wool—in sweaters and blankets, filters, flame-resistant awnings, tents, artificial fur, and children's sleepwear.

(*Below*) In the summer of 1952 "wash and wear" was coined to describe a new blend of cotton and acrylic. Now everyone expects this as a property of the clothes they wear.

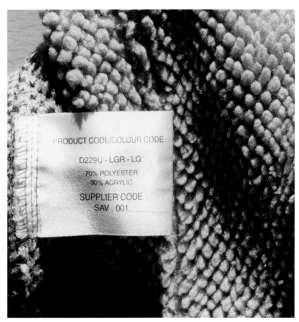

PRODUCT CODE/COLOUR CODE

D229U - LGR - LG

70% POLYESTER
30% ACRYLIC

SUPPLIER CODE
SAV 001

Acrylic fiber

Acrylics are some of the oldest polymers used for fibers. A variation of acrylic plastic was produced in America in 1950 and made into an acrylic fiber called Orlon®. From this began the widespread use of acrylic fibers in clothing.

Acrylics are made by reacting polypropylene with ammonia. The raw material is also known as polyacrylonitrile, or PAN. This material is difficult to dissolve (and so put through a spinneret) and will not take dyes, so vinyl acetate is added. The resulting mixture is soft and makes fibers easily.

Acrylics are unique among synthetic fibers because they have an uneven surface, even when extruded from a round-hole spinneret. That makes them soft and flexible, with a feel like wool. As a result, most acrylics are used in clothing, upholstery, and carpets as a wool substitute. Acrylics can be made and the products sold at a very small fraction of the equivalent cost of the natural fiber. They will not rot and are not attacked by insects.

Acrylics are easily washed. They retain their shape and act, as wool does, like natural wicks, transferring moisture from the body to the air. That makes them easy to wear and prevents an unnecessary "clammy" feeling when the body sweats.

Acrylics are often blended with natural fibers such as wool and cotton to make a cheaper garment than one consisting only of pure natural fibers.

When vinyl chloride is added to acrylics, they become significantly more fire-resistant and so can be used for children's clothing and other areas where there is potential fire risk.

Acrylics are prone to the buildup of static electricity on their surfaces.

Acetate fiber

Acetate is made by reacting cellulose from wood pulp with acetic acid. After further chemical treatment (known as HYDROLYSIS) cellulose acetate is formed, which is soluble in cheap solvents such as acetone.

The acetate is made into fiber by extruding it through a spinneret and drying it in a current of warm air. It was first marketed in 1921 under the name Celanese®.

It became a successful product because it had a silky luster and good crease-resistant properties. It does not shrink when washed.

Special dyes have had to be developed for acetate since it does not accept dyes ordinarily used for cotton and rayon.

Acetate, with its silky look and crease resistance, was widely used for blouses, dresses, coat and drape linings, and upholstery. It was also used as the material for cigarette filters. Its use has declined a little since the midtwentieth century because of competition from polyester fiber, which has similar properties but is less expensive to make.

(*Above*) A shiny acetate fiber finish makes this a suitable silk substitute often used to line suits and jackets. Common or trade names for acetate fibers include Tricel® and Arnel®.

Microfiber

People have long treasured the fineness of some natural fibers in making fabrics. However, naturally fine fibers are scarce, and until recently it has not been possible to make very fine man-made fibers. In fiber terms a very fine fiber is less than 1 denier (1 g weight per 9,000 m of fiber). This kind of fiber, which is finer than silk, is called a microfiber. Most new microfibers are made of polyester.

The advantages of a microfiber are often in lightness. For example, rainwear made of microfibers will still let moist air pass through, but it will be much thinner than conventional fabric and so is lighter and more comfortable to wear (see also page 18).

Of course, a thinner fiber is liable to be weaker than a thicker fiber, so special care has to be taken to make microfibers very strong. Microfibers are not suitable as insulating fibers because they do not trap much air.

Microfiber

Microfiber is finer than silk, which is the finest natural fiber.

Nylon

Nylon, so called because it was a collaborative effort between teams in <u>N</u>ew <u>Y</u>ork and <u>Lon</u>don, is not a single product but a family of fabrics called POLYAMIDES (a chain of amides).

Each form of nylon is made by causing an acid and another chemical called an amine to join in chains of compounds called amides. (For a representation of a typical reaction to create nylon, see page 14. For a laboratory demonstration showing nylon being made, see pages 32 and 33.)

To make nylon, the acid and the amine (a base) are reacted to produce a salt called nylon salt. It is dried and heated under vacuum to remove water. The polymer is turned into a filament by melting it and then forcing it through a spinneret.

Nylon is exceptionally strong, elastic, and resistant to wear—especially from scuffing by shoes. It has a sheen, is easy to wash, does not easily react with other chemicals, and is not easily damaged. It can also be dyed either in the melted state or when made into a filament. Nylon does not absorb water, and it feels reasonably soft, warm, and lightweight.

(*Above*) The strength of nylon is demonstrated in its use for hook and loop fasteners.

(*Right*) Strong open-weave fabrics can be made of nylon and are often used as scouring pads.

(*Left, below left, and right*) When treated with waterproofing, nylon is used for outdoor gear because of its durability. Nylon is also used for toothbrush bristles and for some hot-air balloons.

(*Above and below*) Car safety belts and soft-sided luggage are often made from nylon.

(*Below*) Nylon rope and nylon pile carpet.

Nylon is used for dresses and hosiery (nylon stockings and tights), raincoats, outdoor wear, carpets and drapes, in tire cord, for seat belts and hoses, for parachutes, ropes, nets, thread, fishing line, dental floss, and much much more.

Nylon has a low melting point and so has to be warm washed and ironed at a low temperature.

The various synthetic polyamides (nylons) are usually distinguished from each other by names based on the number of carbon atoms contained in their building blocks. As with polyesters, polyamides are formed by step-growth polymerization of monomers having two reactive groups. Here the reactive functions are acids and amines. The monomers used may have their two reactive functions of the same chemical type (both acids or both amines) or of different types.

(*Left and below*) Strength and resistance to rotting make nylon a common choice for nets, fishing line, and rope.

(*Right*) Space suits contain multiple layers of nylon fabrics.

(*Above and right*) This photograph shows Kevlar fibers embedded in the material at the back of the wing of a microlight. This part of the wing experiences the greatest forces and so has the risk of tearing in severe weather conditions.

An American research chemist, Stephanie Kwoleck, discovered a solvent that could make Kevlar aramid fiber. Kevlar threads are stronger than steel, yet very light and are used in many applications where these properties are useful, such as in aircraft, spacecraft, and bulletproof vests.

Nylon 6 is made from building blocks having six carbons in the chain, but with an amine at one end and an acid at the other. Thus only one form of monomer is needed to conduct the reaction.

Nylon 6,6—another very common fiber polymer—is made by reacting molecules of adipic acid (containing six carbons in a chain) with the amine hexamethylenediamine (also six carbon atoms). A representation of this reaction is shown on page 14. In another variant a diamine containing ten carbon atoms is used, and so on.

As with the polyesters, nylons have regular structures, and that allows good interchain forces that give the nylon its high strength.

Both nylon 6 and nylon 6,6 have melting points similar to PET. Also, since the nylon chains are held together with hydrogen bonding, nylons can take up water. This allows them to be dyed from solutions in water, unlike their polyester counterparts.

The aramids are another form of polyamide, in this case containing rings of atoms as part of their chain. That gives them exceptionally great strength and a high melting point. However, they are expensive to make. Kevlar® is typical of a special high-strength variety of nylon.

Polyurethane

Polyurethane is made by a reaction of the chemicals polyols and polyisocyanates. The reaction is designed to form two types of building block—one rigid, the other one elastic. The elastic sections stretch, while the rigid ones give the fiber a shape. This kind of stretchable fiber is called spandex.

(*Left and right*) Polyurethane fibers known as spandex are used in stretch fabrics such as supporting leg and wrist bandages, in sportswear, and in swimsuits. Lycra®, Numa®, Spandelle®, and Vyrene® are common trade names for spandex. Very often a fabric needs only a small proportion of these fibers to give it sufficient stretch. Spandex is often coated with nylon to give better durability.

Olefin fibers

Olefins are a group of synthetic fibers of which the two most important are polypropylene (PP) and polyethylene (PE). Both products are made using propylene and ethylene gases.

All olefin fibers are practically inert, and they do not absorb water. As a result, any chemicals on the surface (stains) can often be removed simply with warm, soapy water. Polypropylene is more useful than polyethylene because it has a higher melting point. However, the melting point of both materials is low. Furthermore, neither type of fiber can be dyed, so the color has to be introduced into the polymer before it is spun.

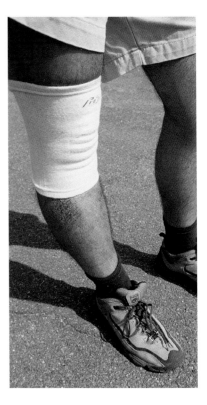

Olefins have good low-static properties, they wear well, they are colorfast (because the color is in the fiber), and they dry quickly because they do not absorb moisture. They resist dirt and stains, and do not deteriorate in sunlight. They are good at being natural wicks, carrying body moisture to the surface, where it evaporates. They feel very comfortable to wear and are the lightest-weight fiber available.

4: Special fibers

Compared to the production of fibers for fabrics, all other fiber production is small. Nevertheless, some very important fibers are made for specific purposes. Fibers made from glass and carbon are especially important.

Most special fibers are made to perform a particular function that natural and petroleum-based synthetic fibers cannot. This usually relates to strength, heat, and chemical resistance, and also, in the case of optical fibers, to transparency and the ability to hold light inside a fine fiber.

Glass fiber

Glass fibers do not have a very long history even though they are the oldest special purpose fiber to be produced.

(*Right and below*) Glass fiber is a mineral material embedded in a resin to give the brittle resin greater strength.

(*Below and right*) Fishing rods and kayak hulls are commonly made from glass fiber.

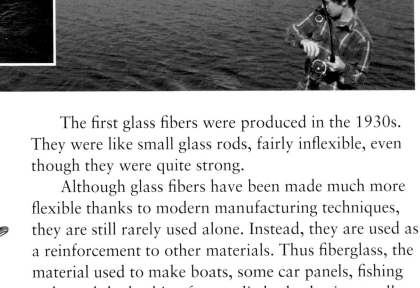

(*Below and right*) Fishing rods and kayak hulls are commonly made from glass fiber.

The first glass fibers were produced in the 1930s. They were like small glass rods, fairly inflexible, even though they were quite strong.

Although glass fibers have been made much more flexible thanks to modern manufacturing techniques, they are still rarely used alone. Instead, they are used as a reinforcement to other materials. Thus fiberglass, the material used to make boats, some car panels, fishing rods, and the backing for acrylic bathtubs, is actually a mixture of polyester and glass fibers set in a RESIN.

Glass is also used in places where resistance to heat is important.

(*Left*) Glass fiber matting is fire resistant.

(*Right*) Glass fiber can be bulked up and used to trap air and so make insulation matting in roof spaces. Its fire resistance makes it preferable in this situation to other kinds of fiber.

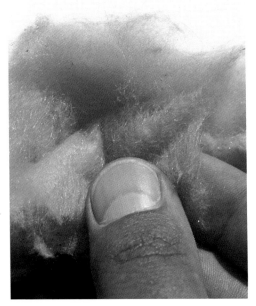

Optical glass fibers

The most significant development in glass-fiber manufacture in recent years has been making optical-quality glass in fiber form.

Glass fibers are used for sending digital telecommunications. A laser light is used as a source. As the light moves down the fiber, it bounces against the sides of the fiber. However, because it always hits the sides of the glass at a low angle, the light is always reflected back into the glass, and it never escapes, even when the glass is bent.

Optical fibers, including their protective glass sheathing, are just over the width of a hair, some 125 microns (millionths of a meter) across, with the transmission fiber being about 10 microns across.

The first glass fibers were made of glass that contained impurities, and they had very limited use. But by the 1960s the glass was of sufficient purity to allow infrared light to be used as a source of information over long distances. Some plastic fibers are also used as optical fibers for short lengths of fiber, but they do not have the high reflecting properties of glass and absorb the light quite quickly.

(*Above*) Glass fiber keeps light inside because the light always strikes the side of the glass at more than the critical angle and is always reflected back inside the glass.

The actual light-carrying fiber is enclosed in a sheath of glass with a different reflectivity to ensure no light gets out.

(*Below*) Light passing through optical fibers.

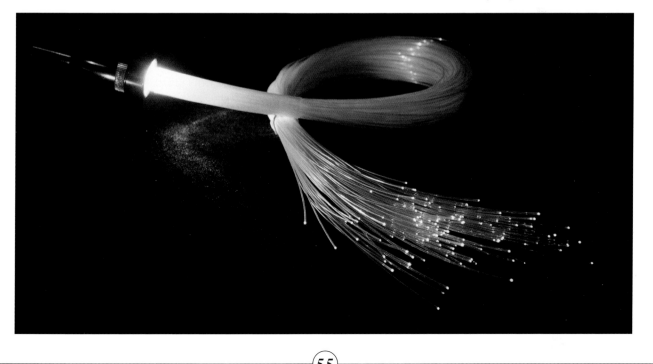

55

The sources of light are either light-emitting diodes (LEDs) or transistor lasers.

Optical fibers are immune to the interference that electrical signals suffer from, and so they are the preferred way of sending digital information. Optical cables are also thinner and lighter than the equivalent electric wires. Most of the main trunk communication links for a national telephone system are now optical rather than electrical. A standard optical cable can send 2.4 gigabits (thousand million) per second per fiber (but the data rate is increasing year by year). A booster is only needed to strengthen the light every 30 km or so. They are entirely optical amplifiers using the element erbium and no electronic components at all.

Visible light is only sent along fiber optic cables for short-distance work such as for medical examination of the body. In this case some of the fibers are used as an elongated lens, while others act as a way of getting illuminated light to the point to be investigated.

Carbon fibers

Although glass, like most synthetic fibers, is an insulator, carbon is a conductor of electricity. All natural and synthetic fibers contain carbon in their structure, but carbon fibers are made almost exclusively of carbon atoms.

When carbon atoms are made into fibers, they can be very strong. The method of production is important in giving carbon fibers their distinctive qualities of flexibility and strength.

Carbon fibers are used like glass fibers to reinforce resins in COMPOSITE MATERIALS. But they can also be made very flexible and given a soft feel so that they can be made into fabrics.

The qualities of a carbon fiber depend on the carbon content (even though all carbon fibers contain more than 90% carbon) and the way the carbon is made into layered sheets within the fiber.

Carbon fibers cannot be made directly from a carbon "solution." Pure carbon is a solid. To make carbon fibers, therefore, the carbon is incorporated in some other fiber and extruded as a filament. The filament is then heated to cause it

(*Above*) Carbon fiber matting.

(Below) Like many pieces of sports equipment, tennis racket heads need to be lightweight. But they also need to stand up to the forces of the nylon strings and the tantrums of the users. Golf club shafts similarly have to withstand huge forces and need to provide a controlled springiness. Carbon-fiber-reinforced resin can be molded into elegant shapes and so suit the sophisticated design demands and fashions expected in modern sporting goods.

(Right) Ski poles, also used for walking, need to be lightweight and strong enough to bear the weight of the user.

to char. Provided the charring is done under conditions of very little oxygen, the charred residue is almost pure carbon. (You can compare this process with the way that charcoal is produced by burning wood in a kiln where the air is excluded.)

Charred fibers are exceptionally fragile, and so the fiber is often made up into a fabric before charring. The carbonized fabric then consists of interlaced carbon fibers in mat form.

The fibers used for making the original matting include rayon, whose carbonized matting is widely used as a thermal shield in space vehicles such as the nose and underbelly shield of the Space Shuttle (where the material is protected by thin ceramic tiles).

When acrylics are used, the intention is to produce a higher-strength fiber than that produced from rayon. As the acrylic mat is carbonized, the fibers are put under tension. This makes the carbon atoms more aligned in a single direction. This kind of carbon fiber is used as a reinforcer for plastic composite materials such as those for making airplanes.

Set Glossary

ACID RAIN: Rain that falls after having been contaminated by acid gases produced by power plants, vehicle exhausts, and other man-made sources.

ACIDITY: The tendency of a liquid to behave like an acid, reacting with metals and alkalis.

ADDITION POLYMERIZATION: The building blocks of many plastics (or polymers) are simple molecules called monomers. Monomers can be converted into polymers by making the monomers link to one another to form long chains in head-to-tail fashion. This is called addition polymerization or chain polymerization. It is most often used to link vinyl monomers to produce, for example, PVC, or polyvinyl chloride polymer.
See also **CONDENSATION POLYMERIZATION**

ADHESIVE: Any substance that can hold materials together simply by using some kind of surface attachment. In some cases this is a chemical reaction; in other cases it is a physical attraction between molecules of the adhesive and molecules of the substance it sticks to.

ADOBE: Simple unbaked brick made with mud, straw, and dung. It is dried in the open air. In this form it is very vulnerable to the effects of rainfall and so is most often found in desert areas or alternatively is protected by some waterproof covering, for example, thatch, straw, or reeds.

ALKALI: A base, or substance that can neutralize acids. In glassmaking an alkali is usually potassium carbonate and used as a flux to lower the melting point of the silica.

ALKYD: Any kind of synthetic resin used for protective coatings such as paint.

ALLOY: A metal mixture made up of two or more elements. Most of the elements used to make an alloy are metals. For example, brass is an alloy of copper and zinc, but carbon is an exception and used to make steel from iron.

AMALGAM: An alloy of mercury and one or more other metals. Dentist's filling amalgam traditionally contains mercury, silver, and tin.

AMPHIBIOUS: Adapted to function on both water and land.

AMORPHOUS: Shapeless and having no crystalline form. Glass is an amorphous solid.

ANION: An ion with a negative charge.

ANNEALING: A way of making a metal, alloy, or glass less brittle and more easy to work (more ductile) by heating it to a certain temperature (depending on the metal), holding it at that temperature for a certain time, and then cooling to room temperature.

ANODIZING: A method of plating metal by electrically depositing an oxide film onto the surface of a metal. The main purpose is to reduce corrosion.

ANTICYCLONE: A region of the Earth's atmosphere where the pressure is greater than average.

AQUEOUS SOLUTION: A substance dissolved in water.

ARTIFACT: An object of a previous time that was created by humans.

ARTIFICIAL DYE: A dye made from a chemical reaction that does not occur in nature. Dyes made from petroleum products are artificial dyes.

ARTIFICIAL FIBER: A fiber made from a material that has been manufactured, and that does not occur naturally. Rayon is an example of an artificial fiber.
Compare to **SYNTHETIC**

ATMOSPHERE: The envelope of gases that surrounds the Earth.

ATOM: The smallest particle of an element; a nucleus and its surrounding electrons.

AZO: A chemical compound that contains two nitrogen atoms joined by a double bond and each linked to a carbon atom. Azon compounds make up more than half of all dyes.

BARK: The exterior protective sheath of the stem and root of a woody plant such as a tree or a shrub. Everything beyond the cambium layer.

BAROMETER: An instrument for measuring atmospheric pressure.

BASE METAL: Having a low value and poorer properties than some other metals. Used, for example, when describing coins that contain metals other than gold or silver.

BAST FIBERS: A strong woody fiber that comes from the phloem of plants and is used for rope and similar products. Flax is an example of a bast fiber.

BATCH: A mixture of raw materials or products that are processes in a tank or kiln. This process produces small amounts of material or products and can be contrasted to continuous processes. Batch processing is used to make metals, alloys, glass, plastics, bricks, and other ceramics, dyes, and adhesives.

BAUXITE: A hydrated impure oxide of aluminum. It is the main ore used to obtain aluminum metal. The reddish-brown color of bauxite is caused by impurities of iron oxides.

BINDER: A substance used to make sure the pigment in a paint sticks to the surface it is applied to.

BIOCERAMICS: Ceramic materials that are used for medical and dental purposes, mainly as implants and replacements.

BLAST FURNACE: A tall furnace charged with a mixture of iron ore, coke, and limestone and used for the refining (smelting) of iron ore. The name comes from the strong blast of air used during smelting.

BLOWING: Forming a glass object by blowing into a gob of molten glass to form a bubble on the end of a blowpipe.

BOLL: The part of the cotton seed that contains the cotton fiber.

BOILING POINT: The temperature at which a liquid changes to a vapor. Boiling points change with atmospheric pressure.

BOND: A transfer or a sharing of electrons by two or more atoms. There are a number of kinds of chemical bonds, some very strong, such as covalent bonding and ionic bonding, and others quite weak, as in hydrogen bonding. Chemical bonds form because the linked molecules are more stable than the unlinked atoms from which they are formed.

BOYLE'S LAW: At constant temperature and for a given mass of gas the volume of the gas is inversely proportional to the pressure that builds up.

BRITTLE: Something that has almost no plasticity and so shatters rather than bends when a force is applied.

BULL'S EYE: A piece of glass with concentric rings marking the place where the blowpipe was attached to the glass. It is the central part of a pane of crown glass.

BUOYANCY: The tendency of an object to float if it is less dense than the liquid it is placed in.

BURN: A combustion reaction in which a flame is produced. A flame occurs where gases combust and release heat and light. At least two gases are therefore required if there is to be a flame.

CALORIFIC: Relating to the production of heat.

CAMBIUM: A thin growing layer that separates the xylem and phloem in most plants, and that produces new cell layers.

CAPACITOR: An electronic device designed for the temporary storage of electricity.

CAPILLARY ACTION, CAPILLARITY: The process by which surface tension forces can draw a liquid up a fine-bore tube.

CARBOHYDRATES: One of the main constituents of green plants, containing compounds of carbon, hydrogen, and oxygen. The main kinds of carbohydrate are sugars, starches, and celluloses.

CARBON COMPOUNDS: Any compound that includes the element carbon. Carbon compounds are also called organic compounds because they form an essential part of all living organisms.

CARBON CYCLE: The continuous movement of carbon between living things, the soil, the atmosphere, oceans, and rocks, especially those containing coal and petroleum.

CAST: To pour a liquid metal, glass, or other material into a mold and allow it to cool so that it solidifies and takes on the shape of the mold.

CATALYST: A substance that speeds up a chemical reaction but itself remains unchanged. For example, platinum is used in a catalytic converter of gases in the exhausts leaving motor vehicles.

CATALYTIC EFFECT: The way a substance helps speed up a reaction even though that substance does not form part of the reaction.

CATHODIC PROTECTION: The technique of protecting a metal object by connecting it to a more easily oxidizable material. The metal object being protected is made into the cathode of a cell. For example, iron can be protected by coupling it with magnesium.

CATION: An ion with a positive charge, often a metal.

CELL: A vessel containing two electrodes and a liquid substance that conducts electricity (an electrolyte).

CELLULOSE: A form of carbohydrate. *See* **CARBOHYDRATE**

CEMENT: A mixture of alumina, silica, lime, iron oxide, and magnesium oxide that is burned together in a kiln and then made into a powder. It is used as the main ingredient of mortar and as the adhesive in concrete.

CERAMIC: A crystalline nonmetal. In a more everyday sense it is a material based on clay that has been heated so that it has chemically hardened.

CHARRING: To burn partly so that some of a material turns to carbon and turns black.

CHINA: A shortened version of the original "Chinese porcelain," it also refers to various porcelain objects such as plates and vases meant for domestic use.

CHINA CLAY: The mineral kaolinite, which is a very white clay used as the basis of porcelain manufacture.

CLAY MINERALS: The minerals, such as kaolinite, illite, and montmorillonite, that occur naturally in soils and some rocks, and that are all minute platelike crystals.

COKE: A form of coal that has been roasted in the absence of air to remove much of the liquid and gas content.

COLORANTS: Any substance that adds a color to a material. The pigments in paints and the chemicals that make dyes are colorants.

COLORFAST: A dye that will not "run" in water or change color when it is exposed to sunlight.

COMPOSITE MATERIALS: Materials such as plywood that are normally regarded as a single material, but that themselves are made up of a number of different materials bonded together.

COMPOUND: A chemical consisting of two or more elements chemically bonded together, for example, calcium carbonate.

COMPRESSED AIR: Air that has been squashed to reduce its volume.

COMPRESSION: To be squashed.

COMPRESSION MOLDING: The shaping of an object, such as a headlight lens, which is achieved by squashing it into a mold.

CONCRETE: A mixture of cement and a coarse material such as sand and small stones.

CONDENSATION: The process of changing a gas to a liquid.

CONDENSATION POLYMERIZATION: The production of a polymer formed by a chain of reactions in which a water molecule is eliminated as every link of the polymer is formed. Polyester is an example.

CONDUCTION: (i) The exchange of heat (heat conduction) by contact with another object, or (ii) allowing the flow of electrons (electrical conduction).

CONDUCTIVITY: The property of allowing the flow of heat or electricity.

CONDUCTOR: (i) Heat—a material that allows heat to flow in and out of it easily. (ii) Electricity—a material that allows electrons to flow through it easily.

CONTACT ADHESIVE: An adhesive that, when placed on the surface to be joined, sticks as soon as the surfaces are placed firmly together.

CONVECTION: The circulating movement of molecules in a liquid or gas as a result of heating it from below.

CORRODE/CORROSION: A reaction usually between a metal and an acid or alkali in which the metal decomposes. The word is used in the sense of the metal being eaten away and dangerously thinned.

CORROSIVE: Causing corrosion, that is, the oxidation of a metal. For example, sodium hydroxide is corrosive.

COVALENT BONDING: The most common type of strong chemical bond, which occurs when two atoms share electrons. For example, oxygen O_2.

CRANKSHAFT: A rodlike piece of a machine designed to change linear into rotational motion or vice versa.

CRIMP: To cause to become wavy.

CRUCIBLE: A ceramic-lined container for holding molten metal, glass, and so on.

CRUDE OIL: A chemical mixture of petroleum liquids. Crude oil forms the raw material for an oil refinery.

CRYSTAL: A substance that has grown freely so that it can develop external faces.

CRYSTALLINE: A solid in which the atoms, ions, or molecules are organized into an orderly pattern without distinct crystal faces.

CURING: The process of allowing a chemical change to occur simply by waiting a while. Curing is often a process of reaction with water or with air.

CYLINDER GLASS: An old method of making window glass by blowing a large bubble of glass, then swinging it until it forms a cylinder. The ends of the cylinder are then cut off with shears and the sides of the cylinder allowed to open out until they form a flat sheet.

DECIDUOUS: A plant that sheds its leaves seasonally.

DECOMPOSE: To rot. Decomposing plant matter releases nutrients back to the soil and in this way provides nourishment for a new generation of living things.

DENSITY: The mass per unit volume (for example, g/c^3).

DESICCATE: To dry up thoroughly.

DETERGENT: A cleaning agent that is able to turn oils and dirts into an emulsion and then hold them in suspension so they can be washed away.

DIE: A tool for giving metal a required shape either by striking the object with the die or by forcing the object over or through the die.

DIFFUSION: The slow mixing of one substance with another until the two substances are evenly mixed. Mixing occurs because of differences in concentration within the mixture. Diffusion works rapidly with gases, very slowly with liquids.

DILUTE: To add more of a solvent to a solution.

DISSOCIATE: To break up. When a compound dissociates, its molecules break up into separate ions.

DISSOLVED: To break down a substance in a solution without causing a reaction.

DISTILLATION: The process of separating mixtures by condensing their vapors through cooling. The simplest form of distillation uses a Liebig condenser arranged with just a slight slope down to the collecting vessel. When the liquid mixture is heated and vapors are produced, they enter the water cooled condenser and then flow down the tube, where they can be collected.

DISTILLED WATER: Water that has its dissolved solids removed by the process of distillation.

DOPING: Adding an impurity to the surface of a substance in order to change its properties.

DORMANT: A period of inactivity such as during winter, when plants stop growing.

DRAWING: The process in which a piece of metal is pulled over a former or through dies.

DRY-CLEANED: A method of cleaning fabrics with nonwater-based organic solvents such as carbon tetrachloride.

DUCTILE: Capable of being drawn out or hammered thin.

DYE: A colored substance that will stick to another substance so that both appear to be colored.

EARLY WOOD: The wood growth put on the spring of each year.

EARTHENWARE: Pottery that has not been fired to the point where some of the clay crystals begin to melt and fuse together and is thus slightly porous and coarser than stoneware or porcelain.

ELASTIC: The ability of an object to regain its original shape after it has been deformed.

ELASTIC CHANGE: To change shape elastically.

ELASTICITY: The property of a substance that causes it to return to its original shape after it has been deformed in some way.

ELASTIC LIMIT: The largest force that a material can stand before it changes shape permanently.

ELECTRODE: A conductor that forms one terminal of a cell.

ELECTROLYSIS: An electrical-chemical process that uses an electric current to cause the breakup of a compound and the movement of metal ions in a solution. It is commonly used in industry for purifying (refining) metals or for plating metal objects with a fine, even metal coat.

ELECTROLYTE: An ionic solution that conducts electricity.

ELECTROMAGNET: A temporary magnet that is produced when a current of electricity passes through a coil of wire.

ELECTRON: A tiny, negatively charged particle that is part of an atom. The flow of electrons through a solid material such as a wire produces an electric current.

ELEMENT: A substance that cannot be decomposed into simpler substances by chemical means, for example, silver and copper.

EMULSION: Tiny droplets of one substance dispersed in another.

EMULSION PAINT: A paint made of an emulsion that is water soluble (also called latex paint).

ENAMEL: A substance made of finely powdered glass colored with a metallic oxide and suspended in oil so that it can be applied with a brush. The enamel is then heated, the oil burns away, and the glass fuses. Also used colloquially to refer to certain kinds of resin-based paint that have extremely durable properties.

ENGINEERED WOOD PRODUCTS: Wood products such as plywood sheeting made from a combination of wood sheets, chips or sawdust, and resin.

EVAPORATION: The change of state of a liquid to a gas. Evaporation happens below the boiling point.

EXOTHERMIC REACTION: A chemical reaction that gives out heat.

EXTRUSION: To push a substance through an opening so as to change its shape.

FABRIC: A material made by weaving threads into a network, often just referred to as cloth.

FELTED: Wool that has been hammered in the presence of heat and moisture to change its texture and mat the fibers.

FERRITE: A magnetic substance made of ferric oxide combined with manganese, nickel, or zinc oxide.

FIBER: A long thread.

FILAMENT: (i) The coiled wire used inside a light bulb. It consists of a high-resistance metal such as tungsten that also has a high melting point. (ii) A continuous thread produced during the manufacture of fibers.

FILLER: A material introduced in order to give bulk to a substance. Fillers are used in making paper and also in the manufacture of paints and some adhesives.

FILTRATE: The liquid that has passed through a filter.

FLOOD: When rivers spill over their banks and cover the surrounding land with water.

FLUID: Able to flow either as a liquid or a gas.

FLUORESCENT: A substance that gives out visible light when struck by invisible waves, such as ultraviolet rays.

FLUX: A substance that lowers the melting temperature of another substance. Fluxes are use in glassmaking and in melting alloys. A flux is used, for example, with a solder.

FORMER: An object used to control the shape or size of a product being made, for example, glass.

FOAM: A material that is sufficiently gelatinous to be able to contain bubbles of gas. The gas bulks up the substances, making it behave as though it were semirigid.

FORGE: To hammer a piece of heated metal until it changes to the desired shape.

FRACTION: A group of similar components of a mixture. In the petroleum industry the light fractions of crude oil are those with the smallest molecules, while the medium and heavy fractions have larger molecules.

FRACTIONAL DISTILLATION: The separation of the components of a liquid mixture by heating them to their boiling points.

FREEZING POINT: The temperature at which a substance undergoes a phase change from a liquid to a solid. It is the same temperature as the melting point.

FRIT: Partly fused materials of which glass is made.

FROTH SEPARATION: A process in which air bubbles are blown through a suspension, causing a froth of bubbles to collect on the surface. The materials that are attracted to the bubbles can then be removed with the froth.

FURNACE: An enclosed fire designed to produce a very high degree of heat for melting glass or metal or for reheating objects so they can be further processed.

FUSING: The process of melting particles of a material so they form a continuous sheet or solid object. Enamel is bonded to the surface of glass this way. Powder-formed metal is also fused into a solid piece. Powder paints are fused to the surface by heating.

GALVANIZING: The application of a surface coating of zinc to iron or steel.

GAS: A form of matter in which the molecules take no definite shape and are free to move around to uniformly fill any vessel they are put in. A gas can easily be compressed into a much smaller volume.

GIANT MOLECULES: Molecules that have been formed by polymerization.

GLASS: A homogeneous, often transparent material with a random noncrystalline molecular structure. It is achieved by cooling a molten substance very rapidly so that it cannot crystallize.

GLASS CERAMIC: A ceramic that is not entirely crystalline.

GLASSY STATE: A solid in which the molecules are arranged randomly rather than being formed into crystals.

GLOBAL WARMING: The progressive increase in the average temperature of the Earth's atmosphere, most probably in large part due to burning fossil fuels.

GLUE: An adhesive made from boiled animal bones.

GOB: A piece of near-molten glass used by glass-blowers and in machines to make hollow glass vessels.

GRAIN: (i) The distinctive pattern of fibers in wood. (ii) Small particles of a solid, including a single crystal.

GRAPHITE: A form of the element carbon with a sheetlike structure.

GRAVITY: The attractive force produced because of the mass of an object.

GREENHOUSE EFFECT: An increase in the global air temperature as a result of heat released from burning fossil fuels being absorbed by carbon dioxide in the atmosphere.

GREENHOUSE GAS: Any of various gases that contribute to the greenhouse effect, such as carbon dioxide.

GROUNDWATER: Water that flows naturally through rocks as part of the water cycle.

GUM: Any natural adhesive of plant origin that consists of colloidal polysaccharide substances that are gelatinous when moist but harden on drying.

HARDWOOD: The wood from a nonconiferous tree.

HEARTWOOD: The old, hard, nonliving central wood of trees.

HEAT: The energy that is transferred when a substance is at a different temperature than that of its surroundings.

HEAT CAPACITY: The ratio of the heat supplied to a substance compared with the rise in temperature that is produced.

HOLOGRAM: A three-dimensional image reproduced from a split laser beam.

HYDRATION: The process of absorption of water by a substance. In some cases hydration makes a substance change color, but in all cases there is a change in volume.

HYDROCARBON: A compound in which only hydrogen and carbon atoms are present. Most fuels are hydrocarbons, for example, methane.

HYDROFLUORIC ACID: An extremely corrosive acid that attacks silicate minerals such as glass. It is used to etch decoration onto glass and also to produce some forms of polished surface.

HYDROGEN BOND: A type of attractive force that holds one molecule to another. It is one of the weaker forms of intermolecular attractive force.

HYDROLYSIS: A reversible process of decomposition of a substance in water.

HYDROPHILIC: Attracted to water.

HYDROPHOBIC: Repelled by water.

IMMISCIBLE: Will not mix with another substance, for example, oil and water.

IMPURITIES: Any substances that are found in small quantities, and that are not meant to be in the solution or mixture.

INCANDESCENT: Glowing with heat, for example, a tungsten filament in a light bulb.

INDUSTRIAL REVOLUTION: The time, which began in the 18th century and continued through into the 19th century, when materials began to be made with the use of power machines and mass production.

INERT: A material that does not react chemically.

INORGANIC: A substance that does not contain the element carbon (and usually hydrogen), for example, sodium chloride.

INSOLUBLE: A substance that will not dissolve, for example, gold in water.

INSULATOR: A material that does not conduct electricity.

ION: An atom or group of atoms that has gained or lost one or more electrons and so developed an electrical charge.

IONIC BONDING: The form of bonding that occurs between two ions when the ions have opposite charges, for example, sodium ions bond with chloride ions to make sodium chloride. Ionic bonds are strong except in the presence of a solvent.

IONIZE: To change into ions.

ISOTOPE: An atom that has the same number of protons in its nucleus, but that has a different mass, for example, carbon 12 and carbon 14.

KAOLINITE: A form of clay mineral found concentrated as china clay. It is the result of the decomposition of the mineral feldspar.

KILN: An oven used to heat materials. Kilns at quite low temperatures are used to dry wood and at higher temperatures to bake bricks and to fuse enamel onto the surfaces of other substances. They are a form of furnace.

KINETIC ENERGY: The energy due to movement. When a ball is thrown, it has kinetic energy.

KNOT: The changed pattern in rings in wood due to the former presence of a branch.

LAMINATE: An engineered wood product consisting of several wood layers bonded by a resin. Also applies to strips of paper stuck together with resins to make such things as "formica" worktops.

LATE WOOD: Wood produced during the summer part of the growing season.

LATENT HEAT: The amount of heat that is absorbed or released during the process of changing state between gas, liquid, or solid. For example, heat is absorbed when liquid changes to gas. Heat is given out again as the gas condenses back to a liquid.

LATEX: A general term for a colloidal suspension of rubber-type material in water. Originally for the milky white liquid emulsion found in the Para rubber tree, but also now any manufactured water emulsion containing synthetic rubber or plastic.

LATEX PAINT: A water emulsion of a synthetic rubber or plastic used as paint. *See* **EMULSION PAINT**

LATHE: A tool consisting of a rotating spindle and cutters that is designed to produce shaped objects that are symmetrical about the axis of rotation.

LATTICE: A regular geometric arrangement of objects in space.

LEHR: The oven used for annealing glassware. It is usually a very long tunnel through which glass passes on a conveyor belt.

LIGHTFAST: A colorant that does not fade when exposed to sunlight.

LIGNIN: A form of hard cellulose that forms the walls of cells.

LIQUID: A form of matter that has a fixed volume but no fixed shape.

LUMBER: Timber that has been dressed for use in building or carpentry and consists of planed planks.

MALLEABLE: Capable of being hammered or rolled into a new shape without fracturing due to brittleness.

MANOMETER: A device for measuring liquid or gas pressure.

MASS: The amount of matter in an object. In common use the word weight is used instead (incorrectly) to mean mass.

MATERIAL: Anything made of matter.

MATTED: Another word for felted. *See* **FELTED**

MATTER: Anything that has mass and takes up space.

MELT: The liquid glass produced when a batch of raw materials melts. Also used to describe molten metal.

MELTING POINT: The temperature at which a substance changes state from a solid phase to a liquid phase. It is the same as the freezing point.

METAL: A class of elements that is a good conductor of electricity and heat, has a metallic luster, is malleable and ductile, and is formed as cations held together by a sea of electrons. A metal may also be an alloy of these elements and carbon.

METAL FATIGUE: The gradual weakening of a metal by constant bending until a crack develops.

MINERAL: A solid substance made of just one element or compound, for example, calcite minerals contain only calcium carbonate.

MISCIBLE: Capable of being mixed.

MIXTURE: A material that can be separated into two or more substances using physical means, for example, air.

MOLD: A containing shape made of wood, metal, or sand into which molten glass or metal is poured. In metalworking it produces a casting. In glassmaking the glass is often blown rather than poured when making, for example, light bulbs.

MOLECULE: A group of two or more atoms held together by chemical bonds.

MONOMER: A small molecule and building block for larger chain molecules or polymers (mono means "one" and mer means "part").

MORDANT: A chemical that is attracted to a dye and also to the surface that is to be dyed.

MOSAIC: A decorated surface made from a large number of small colored pieces of glass, natural stone, or ceramic that are cemented together.

NATIVE METAL: A pure form of a metal not combined as a compound. Native metals are more common in nonreactive elements such as gold than reactive ones such as calcium.

NATURAL DYES: Dyes made from plants without any chemical alteration, for example, indigo.

NATURAL FIBERS: Fibers obtained from plants or animals, for example, flax and wool.

NEUTRON: A particle inside the nucleus of an atom that is neutral and has no charge.

NOBLE GASES: The members of group 8 of the periodic table of the elements: helium, neon, argon, krypton, xenon, radon. These gases are almost entirely unreactive.

NONMETAL: A brittle substance that does not conduct electricity, for example, sulfur or nitrogen.

OIL-BASED PAINTS: Paints that are not based on water as a vehicle. Traditional artists' oil paint uses linseed oil as a vehicle.

OPAQUE: A substance through which light cannot pass.

ORE: A rock containing enough of a useful substance to make mining it worthwhile, for example, bauxite, the ore of aluminum.

ORGANIC: A substance that contains carbon and usually hydrogen. The carbonates are usually excluded.

OXIDE: A compound that includes oxygen and one other element, for example, Cu_2O, copper oxide.

OXIDIZE, OXIDIZING AGENT: A reaction that occurs when a substance combines with oxygen or a reaction in which an atom, ion, or molecule loses electrons to another substance (and in this more general case does not have to take up oxygen).

OZONE: A form of oxygen whose molecules contain three atoms of oxygen. Ozone high in the atmosphere blocks harmful ultraviolet rays from the Sun, but at ground level it is an irritant gas when breathed in and so is regarded as a form of pollution. The ozone layer is the uppermost part of the stratosphere.

PAINT: A coating that has both decorative and protective properties, and that consists of a pigment suspended in a vehicle, or binder, made of a resin dissolved in a solvent. It dries to give a tough film.

PARTIAL PRESSURE: The pressure a gas in a mixture would exert if it alone occupied the flask. For example, oxygen makes up about a fifth of the atmosphere. Its partial pressure is therefore about a fifth of normal atmospheric pressure.

PASTE: A thick suspension of a solid in a liquid.

PATINA: A surface coating that develops on metals and protects them from further corrosion, for example, the green coating of copper carbonate that forms on copper statues.

PERIODIC TABLE: A chart organizing elements by atomic number and chemical properties into groups and periods.

PERMANENT HARDNESS: Hardness in the water that cannot be removed by boiling.

PETROCHEMICAL: Any of a large group of manufactured chemicals (not fuels) that come from petroleum and natural gas. It is usually taken to include similar products that can be made from coal and plants.

PETROLEUM: A natural mixture of a range of gases, liquids, and solids derived from the decomposed remains of animals and plants.

PHASE: A particular state of matter. A substance can exist as a solid, liquid, or gas and may change between these phases with the addition or removal of energy, usually in the form of heat.

PHOSPHOR: A material that glows when energized by ultraviolet or electron beams, such as in fluorescent tubes and cathode ray tubes.

PHOTOCHEMICAL SMOG: A mixture of tiny particles of dust and soot combined with a brown haze caused by the reaction of colorless nitric oxide from vehicle exhausts and oxygen of the air to form brown nitrogen dioxide.

PHOTOCHROMIC GLASSES: Glasses designed to change color with the intensity of light. They use the property that certain substances, for example, silver halide, can change color (and change chemically) in light. For example, when silver chromide is dispersed in the glass melt, sunlight decomposes the silver halide to release silver (and so darken the lens). But the halogen cannot escape; and when the light is removed, the halogen recombines with the silver to turn back to colorless silver halide.

PHOTOSYNTHESIS: The natural process that happens in green plants whereby the energy from light is used to help turn gases, water, and minerals into tissue and energy.

PIEZOELECTRICS: Materials that produce electric currents when they are deformed, or vice versa.

PIGMENT: Insoluble particles of coloring material.

PITH: The central strand of spongy tissue found in the stems of most plants.

PLASTIC: Material—a carbon-based substance consisting of long chains or networks (polymers) of simple molecules. The word plastic is commonly used only for synthetic polymers. Property—a material is plastic if it can be made to change shape easily and then remain in this new shape (contrast with elasticity and brittleness).

PLASTIC CHANGE: A permanent change in shape that happens without breaking.

PLASTICIZER: A chemical added to rubbers and resins to make it easier for them to be deformed and molded. Plasticizers are also added to cement to make it more easily worked when used as a mortar.

PLATE GLASS: Rolled, ground, and polished sheet glass.

PLIABLE: Supple enough to be repeatedly bent without fracturing.

PLYWOOD: An engineered wood laminate consisting of sheets of wood bonded with resin. Each sheet of wood has the grain at right angles to the one above and below. This imparts stability to the product.

PNEUMATIC DEVICE: Any device that works with air pressure.

POLAR: Something that has a partial electric charge.

POLYAMIDES: A compound that contains more than one amide group, for example, nylon.

POLYMER: A compound that is made of long chains or branching networks by combining molecules called monomers as repeating units. Poly means "many," mer means "part."

PORCELAIN: A hard, fine-grained, and translucent white ceramic that is made of china clay and is fired to a high temperature. Varieties include china.

PORES: Spaces between particles that are small enough to hold water by capillary action, but large enough to allow water to enter.

POROUS: A material that has small cavities in it, known as pores. These pores may or may not be joined. As a result, porous materials may or may not allow a liquid or gas to pass through them. Popularly, porous is used to mean permeable, the kind of porosity in which the pores are joined, and liquids or gases can flow.

POROUS CERAMICS: Ceramics that have not been fired at temperatures high enough to cause the clays to fuse and so prevent the slow movement of water.

POTENTIAL ENERGY: Energy due to the position of an object. Water in a reservoir has potential energy because it is stored up, and when released, it moves down to a lower level.

POWDER COATING: The application of a pigment in powder form without the use of a solvent.

POWDER FORMING: A process of using a powder to fill a mold and then heating the powder to make it fuse into a solid.

PRECIPITATE: A solid substance formed as a result of a chemical reaction between two liquids or gases.

PRESSURE: The force per unit area measured in SI units in Pascals and also more generally in atmospheres.

PRIMARY COLORS: A set of colors from which all others can be made. In transmitted light they are red, blue, and green.

PROTEIN: Substances in plants and animals that include nitrogen.

PROTON: A positively charged particle in the nucleus of an atom that balances out the charge of the surrounding electrons.

QUENCH: To put into water in order to cool rapidly.

RADIATION: The transmission of energy from one body to another without any contribution from the intervening space. *Contrast with* **CONVECTION** and **CONDUCTION**

RADIOACTIVE: A substance that spontaneously emits energetic particles.

RARE EARTHS: Any of a group of metal oxides that are found widely throughout the Earth's rocks, but in low concentrations. They are mainly made up of the elements of the lanthanide series of the periodic table of the elements.

RAW MATERIAL: A substance that has not been prepared, but that has an intended use in manufacturing.

RAY: Narrow beam of light.

RAYON: An artificial fiber made from natural cellulose.

REACTION (CHEMICAL): The recombination of two substances using parts of each substance.

REACTIVE: A substance that easily reacts with many other substances.

RECYCLE: To take once used materials and make them available for reuse.

REDUCTION, REDUCING AGENT: The removal of oxygen from or the addition of hydrogen to a compound.

REFINING: Separating a mixture into the simpler substances of which it is made, especially petrochemical refining.

REFRACTION: The bending of a ray of light as it passes between substances of different refractive index (light-bending properties).

REFRACTORY: Relating to the use of a ceramic material, especially a brick, in high-temperature conditions of, for example, a furnace.

REFRIGERANT: A substance that, on changing between a liquid and a gas, can absorb large amounts of (latent) heat from its surroundings.

REGENERATED FIBERS: Fibers that have been dissolved in a solution and then recovered from the solution in a different form.

REINFORCED FIBER: A fiber that is mixed with a resin, for example, glass-reinforced fiber.

RESIN: A semisolid natural material that is made of plant secretions and often yellow-brown in color. Also synthetic

materials with the same type of properties. Synthetic resins have taken over almost completely from natural resins and are available as thermoplastic resins and thermosetting resins.

RESPIRATION: The process of taking in oxygen and releasing carbon dioxide in animals and the reverse in plants.

RIVET: A small rod of metal that is inserted into two holes in metal sheets and then burred over at both ends in order to stick the sheets together.

ROCK: A naturally hard inorganic material composed of mineral particles or crystals.

ROLLING: The process in which metal is rolled into plates and bars.

ROSIN: A brittle form of resin used in varnishes.

RUST: The product of the corrosion of iron and steel in the presence of air and water.

SALT: Generally thought of as sodium chloride, common salt; however, more generally a salt is a compound involving a metal. There are therefore many "salts" in water in addition to sodium chloride.

SAPWOOD: The outer, living layers of the tree, which includes cells for the transportation of water and minerals between roots and leaves.

SATURATED: A state in which a liquid can hold no more of a substance dissolved in it.

SEALANTS: A material designed to stop water or other liquids from penetrating into a surface or between surfaces. Most sealants are adhesives.

SEMICONDUCTOR: A crystalline solid that has an electrical conductivity part way between a conductor and an insulator. This material can be altered by doping to control an electric current. Semiconductors are the basis of transistors, integrated circuits, and other modern electronic solid-state devices.

SEMIPERMEABLE MEMBRANE: A thin material that acts as a fine sieve or filter, allowing small molecules to pass, but holding back large molecules.

SEPARATING COLUMN: A tall glass tube containing a porous disk near the base and filled with a substance such as aluminum oxide that can absorb materials on its surface. When a mixture passes through the columns, fractions are retarded by differing amounts so that each fraction is washed through the column in sequence.

SEPARATING FUNNEL: A pear-shaped glass funnel designed to permit the separation of immiscible liquids by simply pouring off the more dense liquid from the bottom of the funnel, while leaving the less dense liquid in the funnel.

SHAKES: A defect in wood produced by the wood tissue separating, usually parallel to the rings.

SHEEN: A lustrous, shiny surface on a yarn. It is produced by the finishing process or may be a natural part of the yarn.

SHEET-METAL FORMING: The process of rolling out metal into sheet.

SILICA: Silicon dioxide, most commonly in the form of sand.

SILICA GLASS: Glass made exclusively of silica.

SINTER: The process of heating that makes grains of a ceramic or metal a solid mass before it becomes molten.

SIZE: A glue, varnish, resin, or similar very dilute adhesive sealant used to block up the pores in porous surfaces or, for example, plaster and paper. Once the size has dried, paint or other surface coatings can be applied without the coating sinking in.

SLAG: A mixture of substances that are waste products of a furnace. Most slag are mainly composed of silicates.

SMELTING: Roasting a substance in order to extract the metal contained in it.

SODA: A flux for glassmaking consisting of sodium carbonate.

SOFTWOOD: Wood obtained from a coniferous tree.

SOLID: A rigid form of matter that maintains its shape regardless of whether or not it is in a container.

SOLIDIFICATION: Changing from a liquid to a solid.

SOLUBILITY: The maximum amount of a substance that can be contained in a solvent.

SOLUBLE: Readily dissolvable in a solvent.

SOLUTION: A mixture of a liquid (the solvent) and at least one other substance of lesser abundance (the solute). Like all mixtures, solutions can be separated by physical means.

SOLVAY PROCESS: Modern method of manufacturing the industrial alkali sodium carbonate (soda ash).

SOLVENT: The main substance in a solution.

SPECTRUM: A progressive series arranged in order, for example, the range of colors that make up visible light as seen in a rainbow.

SPINNERET: A small metal nozzle perforated with many small holes through which a filament solution is forced. The filaments that emerge are solidified by cooling and the filaments twisted together to form a yarn.

SPINNING: The process of drawing out and twisting short fibers, for example, wool, and thus making a thread or yarn.

SPRING: A natural flow of water from the ground.

STABILIZER: A chemical that, when added to other chemicals, prevents further reactions. For example, in soda lime glass the lime acts as a stabilizer for the silica.

STAPLE: A short fiber that has to be twisted with other fibers (spun) in order to make a long thread or yarn.

STARCHES: One form of carbohydrate. Starches can be used to make adhesives.

STATE OF MATTER: The physical form of matter. There are three states of matter: liquid, solid, and gas.

STEAM: Water vapor at the boiling point of water.

STONEWARE: Nonwhite pottery that has been fired at a high temperature until some of the clay has fused, a state called vitrified. Vitrification makes the pottery impervious to water. It is used for general tableware, often for breakfast crockery.

STRAND: When a number of yarns are twisted together, they make a strand. Strands twisted together make a rope.

SUBSTANCE: A type of material including mixtures.

SULFIDE: A compound that is composed only of metal and sulfur atoms, for example, PbS, the mineral galena.

SUPERCONDUCTORS: Materials that will conduct electricity with virtually no resistance if they are cooled to temperatures close to absolute zero (−273°C).

SURFACE TENSION: The force that operates on the surface of a liquid, and that makes it act as though it were covered with an invisible elastic film.

SURFACTANT: A substance that acts on a surface, such as a detergent.

SUSPENDED, SUSPENSION: Tiny particles in a liquid or a gas that do not settle out with time.

SYNTHETIC: Something that does not occur naturally but has to be manufactured. Synthetics are often produced from materials that do not occur in nature, for example, from petrochemicals. (i) Dye—a synthetic dye is made from petrochemicals, as opposed to natural dyes that are made of extracts of plants. (ii) Fiber—synthetic is a subdivision of artificial. Although both polyester and rayon are artificial fibers, rayon is made from reconstituted natural cellulose fibers and so is not synthetic, while polyester is made from petrochemicals and so is a synthetic fiber.

TANNIN: A group of pale-yellow or light-brown substances derived from plants that are used in dyeing fabric and making ink. Tannins are soluble in water and produce dark-blue or dark-green solutions when added to iron compounds.

TARNISH: A coating that develops as a result of the reaction between a metal and the substances in the air. The most common form of tarnishing is a very thin transparent oxide coating, such as occurs on aluminum. Sulfur compounds in the air make silver tarnish black.

TEMPER: To moderate or to make stronger: used in the metal industry to describe softening hardened steel or cast iron by reheating at a lower temperature or to describe hardening steel by reheating and cooling in oil; or in the glass industry, to describe toughening glass by first heating it and then slowly cooling it.

TEMPORARILY HARD WATER: Hard water that contains dissolved substances that can be removed by boiling.

TENSILE (PULLING STRENGTH): The greatest lengthwise (pulling) stress a substance can bear without tearing apart.

TENSION: A state of being pulled. Compare to compression.

TERRA COTTA: Red earth-colored glazed or unglazed fired clay whose origins lie in the Mediterranean region of Europe.

THERMOPLASTIC: A plastic that will soften and can be molded repeatedly into different shapes. It will then set into the molded shape as it cools.

THERMOSET: A plastic that will set into a molded shape as it first cools, but that cannot be made soft again by reheating.

THREAD: A long length of filament, group of filaments twisted together, or a long length of short fibers that have been spun and twisted together into a continuous strand.

TIMBER: A general term for wood suitable for building or for carpentry and consisting of roughcut planks. *Compare to* **LUMBER**

TRANSITION METALS: Any of the group of metallic elements (for example, chromium and iron) that belong to the central part of the periodic table of the elements and whose oxides commonly occur in a variety of colors.

TRANSPARENT: Something that will readily let light through, for example, window glass. Compare to translucent, when only some light gets through but an image cannot be seen, for example, greaseproof paper.

TROPOSPHERE: The lower part of the atmosphere in which clouds form. In general, temperature decreases with height.

TRUNK: The main stem of a tree.

VACUUM: Something from which all air has been removed.

VAPOR: The gaseous phase of a substance that is a liquid or a solid at that temperature, for example, water vapor is the gaseous form of water.

VAPORIZE: To change from a liquid to a gas, or vapor.

VENEER: A thin sheet of highly decorative wood that is applied to cheap wood or engineered wood products to improve their appearance and value.

VINYL: Often used as a general name for plastic. Strictly, vinyls are polymers derived from ethylene by removal of one hydrogen atom, for example, PVC, polyvinylchloride.

VISCOSE: A yellow-brown solution made by treating cellulose with alkali solution and carbon disulfide and used to make rayon.

VISCOUS, VISCOSITY: Sticky. Viscosity is a measure of the resistance of a liquid to flow. The higher the viscosity—the more viscous it is—the less easily it will flow.

VITREOUS CHINA: A translucent form of china or porcelain.

VITRIFICATION: To heat until a substance changes into a glassy form and fuses together.

VOLATILE: Readily forms a gas. Some parts of a liquid mixture are often volatile, as is the case for crude oil. This allows them to be separated by distillation.

WATER CYCLE: The continual interchange of water between the oceans, the air, clouds, rain, rivers, ice sheets, soil, and rocks.

WATER VAPOR: The gaseous form of water.

WAVELENGTH: The distance between adjacent crests on a wave. Shorter wavelengths have smaller distances between crests than longer wavelengths.

WAX: Substances of animal, plant, mineral, or synthetic origin that are similar to fats but are less greasy and harder. They form hard films that can be polished.

WEAVING: A way of making a fabric by passing two sets of yarns through one another at right angles to make a kind of tight meshed net with no spaces between the yarns.

WELDING: Technique used for joining metal pieces through intense localized heat. Welding often involves the use of a joining metal such as a rod of steel used to attach steel pieces (arc welding).

WETTING: In adhesive spreading, a term that refers to the complete coverage of an adhesive over a surface.

WETTING AGENT: A substance that is able to cover a surface completely with a film of liquid. It is a substance with a very low surface tension.

WHITE GLASS: Also known as milk glass, it is an opaque white glass that was originally made in Venice and meant to look like porcelain.

WROUGHT IRON: A form of iron that is relatively soft and can be bent without breaking. It contains less than 0.1% carbon.

YARN: A strand of fibers twisted together and used to make textiles.

Set Index